Finding Hayley
Finding Me

Finding Hayley Finding Me

My Life-Changing Journey to Actress Hayley Mills

A True Story of Reclaiming the Self

Helen Le Mesurier

BALBOA.
PRESS
A DIVISION OF HAY HOUSE

Balboa Press books may be ordered through booksellers or by contacting:

Balboa Press
A Division of Hay House
1663 Liberty Drive
Bloomington, IN 47403
www.balboapress.com.au
1-(877) 407-4847

ISBN: 978-1-4525-0503-9 (e)
ISBN: 978-1-4525-0502-2 (sc)

Printed in the United States of America
Balboa Press rev. date: 05/10/2012

For my darling daughter, Gemma Rose,
who lights up my life.

And for Hayley,
who validated me in a way no one else could.

Anything you can do, or dream that you can,
begin it now.
Boldness has power and magic in it.

Goethe

Contents

Foreword ix

Acknowledgements xiii

Introduction xv

Part 1: What's It All About? 1

Part 2: They Said I Couldn't Do It 23

Part 3: An Unlikely Prophecy .45

Part 4: Another Time Another Place 69

Part 5: Unexpected Meetings 97

Part 6: Mountains to Move 117

Part 7: Searching for the Self .139

Part 8: Doubt & Divine Timing 181

Foreword

Helen Le Mesurier is a remarkable woman. Very few people show the commitment and determination to take their lives into their own hands and forge themselves into somebody who has the power and the ability to create their life to be whatever they want to be.

I first met Helen when she came to a personal development seminar I was presenting in Newcastle, Australia in 1995. She then attended several other of my seminars, culminating in the Master Teacher Training courses. These were designed to give people the means and information to be successful in presenting their own workshops and seminars.

After the trainings, she ran ten public workshops in Toronto, New South Wales, based on the work she had learnt. This in itself is an outstanding achievement, because she had no experience as a public speaker, and it can be very challenging standing in front of other people and holding their attention for several hours at a time, if you are not used to it.

She has also studied our Story and Screenwriters' Course and is writing a romantic comedy film script and a biographical book as well.

When you meet Helen, you find you are with someone who is centred and calm, friendly and warm, and very attentive and perceptive. Her whole life is aimed at knowing her own true self and establishing herself in a state of peace and joy. Many other people comment on those qualities, which she exhibits. This of course is a result of all the personal development practices she has committed herself to. I am sure her story will be an inspiration to you.

Now to the subject of her book.

When I was young, I would be taken to the cinema to see Hayley Mills performing in films as a child star. Hayley was, in her own way, a superstar at the time, known all over the world for her remarkable performances in international films. She is the daughter of Sir John Mills, a great favourite actor and also international Oscar-winning star. Hayley was able to successfully move on, from the often-difficult circumstances of being a child actress, to creating her own life.

In this book you will see how these two people, Helen and Hayley, discovered the synchronicity and coincidences that can happen once you commit yourself to your goals. It is a testament to the power of the mind that everyone and anyone, who learns how to do it, can use these powers that we all have. Yes, it's true you require determination and persistence and a great interest in the subject. But this not only gives you the foundation to be able to live your dreams, but also to inspire other people to achieve their dreams and goals as well.

It all really comes back to reclaiming the power of your life for yourself, rather than believing that there is some outside force creating your life for you.

The mind is an amazing tool and we have hardly scratched the surface of its abilities.

In a way, you can liken it to man's little journey to the moon, which, when compared to the vastness of the whole Universe, is so tiny as to be totally insignificant. Our journey to explore our minds, so far, is of similar insignificance. There is a whole universe in you to explore and use to benefit your own life.

I encourage you to read this book carefully and see how one person can make such a difference to their own and others' lives, so then you can do it too.

Michael Domeyko Rowland
Byron Bay, January 2012
www.successlovefreedom.com

Acknowledgements

I wish to acknowledge my loving husband, Geoff, for his love and tolerance while I have been writing this manuscript. I am grateful for all his love and support and that he accepts me where I am spiritually. I look forward to spending lots more quality time with him now that this book is finally completed.

I am so proud to be thanking my daughter, Gemma, for editing this book. My appreciation and admiration for her talent in editing my manuscript is immense. I was constantly amazed by her composition insights and knowledge of grammar that became so evident as she worked her way through it. Book editing is her favoured field of work, and I am so pleased that my book was her baptism into that world.

I also want to mention my mother. She has always supported me where Hayley is concerned—fifty years now. From my covering of my bedroom walls with pictures of her in my youth, to stepping out in the hope of meeting Hayley in my adulthood, my mother has always nurtured me in my love of Hayley.

I also wish to acknowledge my sister Leonie. In her I have a sister who has always been a best friend. She has been so supportive and encouraging through my Hayley journey, and throughout the years with all my ups and downs.

I also acknowledge my dear friend Maz (Marian Waite). We've been friends ever since meeting at Sunday School at age nine. Without her Part Eight of this book would not exist. I am thankful and appreciative of her friendship and generosity, from which stemmed the manifestation of my ultimate dream. Thank you, Maz. I love you.

And of course, I acknowledge and give my gratitude to Hayley Mills. Without her there is no story. I thank her for giving me her blessing to have this story published, as it involves sharing with you, my readers, something very personal of *her* life, as well as mine. Our continuing friendship is a source of delight in my life.

Hayley expressed her concern that I had portrayed her in a glowing way, which she considered she did not deserve. I acknowledge that she is like us all with foibles and regrets, but in my interaction with her I wasn't exposed to any aspects of her that I interpreted as undeserving of my perceptions. I looked for and saw only her magnificence. My experience of her in the beginning was of a kindred spirit. In the end it was of a soul-sister. Most of us don't see ourselves as others do, and Hayley, in her humility, doesn't recognise how very brightly her Light shines out to the world . . . but I experienced it firsthand.

Introduction

This book started as a simple record for my daughter, Gemma, of our meeting with Hayley Mills and why it meant so much to me. I thought it was important to do this in case anything happened that prevented me ever being able to share it with her later in her life, when she would understand more. As she was only four years old at the time, I knew it would fade from her memory unless there was something she could read that accompanied the few treasured photos.

However, as time went on, the story revolving around Hayley developed until there was so much to tell that it turned into this volume. My mother and some of my friends encouraged me to write it for publication as they felt it was a fascinating story and one that others would enjoy reading about and perhaps even benefit from.

I believe there is much in this story to help others in their spiritual journey and personal development as they accompany me on my own journey to Hayley: A journey that took me from being a young Christian girl, needing approval, to a woman of confidence, happy with my new understanding of Life, God, Spirituality, and of myself.

I hope you enjoy travelling through the pages of this story with me and that it helps you to see that life, when fuelled with love, is indeed an exciting adventure. The real adventure begins when you find a dream or purpose and don't let it go.

Dreams do come true—if only we believe with all our heart, mind and soul that everything is possible. It all rests within the power of the mind and acting on its intuition. I know, because it happened to me.

Here is my story . . .

PART ONE

What's It All About?

We sat at the railway station, spellbound; my arms wrapped around Gemma. Her head rested on my shoulder; my head rested back onto hers. I was reeling in the afterglow of a dream come true.

This dream had crept into my soul many years earlier and had taken a course that I could *never* have imagined.

*   *   *

I was an average sort of girl, a typical 'girl next door'. I was fortunate to grow up in a happy family environment with no real dysfunction (except that my mother would lock me in the bathroom to make me finish my porridge). I was the youngest of three daughters to parents Edith and Bert Le Mesurier [photos 1-4]. We lived in a pretty area among the trees and kookaburras in Castlecrag on Middle Harbour on the lower north shore of Sydney. I was moulded from a spirited child into a very placid, easy-going, happy soul, who enjoyed life, my sisters, my family and my friends.

As a child I loved to play 'secretaries'. I would form clubs with my friends and keep records of our activities and proceedings, which I used to type on my Mickey Mouse Club tin typewriter. (I look back on this time and recognise that what I had focused on as a child had manifested in my adult life: I worked as a secretary for twenty years).

It was in late 1961, when I was twelve years old, that the film 'Pollyanna' was released, and I first saw Hayley Mills on the screen. Like thousands of others, I found her captivating. An instant enchantment enveloped me, becoming an attraction that developed into, and would for thirty years prove to be, an unexplainable deep attachment to her, bordering on—no, let's be honest now—*over*-bordering on, a preoccupation with her, unparalleled to anything else in my life.

From as early as the age of thirteen I had spent lots of time in the news agencies, devouring all magazines, looking for articles on her. Eventually, after spending all my pocket money (and, as I grew older, money from my earnings) on relevant magazines, I ended up having collected five thousand pictures of her, together with the accompanying articles. I studied these and lovingly arranged them into many scrapbooks, which I bound together into one large volume. They were kept as treasures in my (by then) old school case. In these days, when still living at home with my parents, I had the choice portraits of Hayley up on my bedroom wall, like any fan worth their salt would! My mother took a photo of the 'Hayley wall' on a slide, and I kept it with the scrapbooks in my school case. This would prove to be most unfortunate for me in the future.

Everyone at school who was associated with me (and even some who weren't) knew of my attachment to Hayley. If anyone saw an article to do with her, they would come running to me saying, "Did you see the pictures of Hayley in the newspaper (or magazine)?" Usually I could answer, "Yes, I've got that." But on the rare occasions when I hadn't seen it, I went all out to acquire it. Sometimes girls would just turn up with pictures or articles for me.

One day at school I remember my close friends, Lori and Maz, having a dispute because they both believed themselves to be my best friend, and when I was confronted by them to clarify which one was indeed my best friend (it's a girl thing), I avoided their challenge by stating that my dearest friend was Hayley. Fortunately, Lori and Maz were not offended by such a statement as they knew only too well of my love for Hayley, and rolled their eyes as if to say "we should have known!" (I'm pleased to be able to say that they are two of my closest friends to this day). 'My dearest friend'—that is how I had grown to understand my sense of bonding to Hayley. But many people felt that way about her:

> What Shirley Temple was to Depression kids, Hayley Mills was to '60s boomer brats. Boys fell for her rambunctious pertness. Girls imagined this lively blue-eyed blonde as their best friend. In her heyday, Hayley Mills received about 10,000 fan letters a month.
>
> *Excerpt from article by Susan Wloszczyna,*
> *'Pollyanna Mills is whistling a happy tune again',*
> *USA Today, 12th May, 1997.*

It *was as if* she *were* my dearest friend. I loved her with a pre-occupation. Many people interpreted my feelings for Hayley as just being a teenage crush, but the reality for me was the feeling that a part of me was missing. I didn't ever try to write to her because of the sense of being just one of thousands. I'd be lost within the crowd. That just didn't feel right. What was different for me was the *intensity* of the sense of attachment, which, throughout the years of my life, had *never* waned.

This wasn't because I had nothing else of interest in my life. In fact, at the age of sixteen I was fortunate to travel on board the liner 'Fairstar' to and from England, with visits to ten European countries. However, even this experience didn't overshadow my attachment to Hayley. In fact my attachment to her grew stronger the more life experience I gained.

As you can imagine, many people had their views and opinions about me. What the driving force was behind this obsessive behaviour of mine where Hayley was concerned was anyone's guess. In all other aspects of my life I seemed to be level headed, balanced and well adjusted. My mother saw my attachment to Hayley as stemming from wanting to be like her, wanting to model myself on her. I was taking lessons in piano and singing and had become involved in musical theatre, landing several leading roles. Mum thought that I saw something of myself in Hayley, but these activities didn't have anything to do with her from *my* perspective.

I could not dispute any of the judgements placed on me over Hayley, for what indeed could it all be about? And yet I *knew* that the perceptions that others held were not what constituted the driving force within me. I *knew* that in the depths of my being I *knew* her, but that sounded daft, so I had no alternative than to just let people say what they would. It sounded daft to me too! It was unexplainable, so I just allowed whatever it was to simply *be*—to exist in me—while I forged on with life, taking this integral part of my being with me.

When I moved to the Central Coast of New South Wales in 1969, my treasured school case containing my 'Hayley collection', and my two favoured dolls from my childhood, came with me. When I again moved in 1974, they again came with me. From time to time I would spend hours looking through the scrapbooks at my beloved Hayley, before stowing them away again. I always had a framed photo of Hayley in my bedroom along with the photos of my other friends. She was always included as such.

My 'twin' cousin, Beth, and I really loved watching Hayley's films together. Beth and I thought of ourselves as twin cousins because we were born only two months apart, and we had grown up very close. We loved the fact that Beth's mother made us identical dresses and that when we wore them together we were actually called 'the twins' [photos 5-6]. On top of this we were also 'double-cousins': Beth's father and my mother were brother and sister, and my father and her mother were brother and sister, so we considered ourselves to be as close as sisters.

It was perhaps for this reason that Beth and I loved 'The Parent Trap' so much. We would spend hours together re-enacting the parts of Susan and Sharon. Beth always wanted to be Susan so I was always Sharon. This role probably suited me better anyway because Sharon, being the more agreeable, obeyed the rules and conformed to people's expectations, whereas Susan was more her own person, which Beth aspired to be.

I had enjoyed seeing all of Hayley's Disney films several times over, although I hadn't had the opportunity of seeing her first film, 'Tiger Bay', at that time. The movie of 'Whistle Down the Wind' was always extra special because Hayley's mother had written the story, and because the storyline touched me having been brought up in a strong Christian environment.

My family was heavily involved in the Anglican Church, with my father being a sought-after church organist and choirmaster. Not only were my parents involved in their local church at Castlecrag, but they also, along with a few of their friends, were the joint-founders of it. Was it any wonder then that I had always imagined marrying a man in Holy Orders? This wasn't an ambition of mine, just a very plausible outcome. I had no special dreams or aspirations. I just expected to grow up and imitate my mother by being a loving wife to some nice, easy-going, attentive man, like my father was, and by being a loving mother to my children.

I did end up finding someone like my father, not in his personality, but rather in his passion for church music. In 1977, at age twenty-seven, I was preparing to marry David, an Anglican Church organist and choirmaster. He was a brilliant organist and church musician with many very high qualifications in this area. My innate expectation to marry a priest didn't appear to have manifested. However, how interesting it is that he later became an Anglican parish priest without any input on my part.

In the process of moving in together and amalgamating our belongings, my 'Hayley collection' was branded unnecessary clutter . . . unnecessary to *him* that was! I was told to grow up and to get rid of it, along with my two treasured Pedigree dolls. I was more unsure of myself than I had realized and therefore was backward in coming forward when it came to speaking up for myself. I feared, and hid from, confrontation. I didn't recognize it at that point in time, but I had given my personal power away in my romantic relationships (I hadn't yet read the book 'Women Who Love Too Much', by Robin Norwood).

David didn't have a malicious bone in his body but he had an artistic temperament with mood swings and depression, which worked very effectively by making me feel it necessary to walk on eggshells around him. I wanted him to be happy with me: I was a people pleaser and needed approval. I'd had plenty of ridicule over my strong attachment to Hayley so I needed to make myself amenable in all other ways.

Unbelievably, like an obedient child, I did as I was told! As David had requested, I left my treasured 'Hayley collection', still in my school case, out with the garbage bin, and delivered my two dolls to the doorstep of St. Vincent de Paul at 9.30 at night. It might seem difficult to comprehend why I would have given David the power to intimidate me and convince me to do something that so obviously went against what I would want to do. This said more about me than it did about him. He was not a man who physically threatened or intimidated me. In fact he was a softly spoken gentleman. But I was convinced that *I* was responsible for his happiness or unhappiness. If I did as he wanted, he was happy. If I didn't do as he wanted, *nobody* was happy, for his displeasure seemed to infiltrate the atmosphere. I just happened to be so super-sensitive to him and his opinions (along with being an accommodating, soft, eager-to-please, naïve, sweet thing) that his moods easily worked on me. I needed to have been in control of my own life and not have allowed someone else to take that role from me—or perhaps more pertinently, I shouldn't have been so weak as to *give* that role to someone else. I was lacking that personal power.

There was a hard lesson for me to learn in this, as it cost me dearly, taking much from me and leaving several big scars over the ensuing years.

Keep your power and do what's right for you, not what someone else says to do.

I tossed and turned during the night, regretting what I had done, and wanted to retrieve my school case and my dolls. The following morning, being woken by the sound of the garbage truck collecting our refuse, I yearned to get up and chase it down the road but knew I couldn't. I wondered where the tip was, thinking I could go and rummage through today's lot in an effort to retrieve my school case. But I had to be at work at 8.30 am and didn't have the time to find out the whereabouts of the garbage destination. Once at work I phoned the St. Vincent de Paul's shop and asked about my dolls, but I was told that they had been snatched up quickly and were no longer available to me, "or anyone"! The terseness of the voice upset me, as did the dismissal I received. I got off the phone and cried. Where was the anticipated Christian charity? I was so hurt by the lady's attitude that I didn't have the emotional strength to find a phone number for the tip (if in fact there even was one).

In throwing out my treasures to please David, I also threw away my true identity, for much of who I was was tied up in the years with Hayley. David was so caught up in his own endeavours (which involved performing and studying, at very high levels, all aspects of church music) that he forgot to take the time to get to know the real Helen. He was oblivious to the fact that part of me was now missing. I was a good actor—I lived my married life covering up my hurt and my true feelings while all the time trying to meet with his approval and to gain his affection. The real Helen would never have met with his approval for he would have frowned upon the extravagant reaction that I had to Hayley. He wanted a logical person who had two feet firmly on the ground, not someone whom he could have described as 'being away with the fairies'.

I'm sure my intuitive side gave me warning, but I paid no heed to it. I was now being the person David wanted me to be. I forfeited my expectation of a demonstrative love so that I would not appear needy to him and irritate him. I sound like such a weak person—and I was, because I did whatever got me approval, what pleased others.

No one of any importance in my life had ever told me to discard my 'Hayley collection' before. I was shocked that David required it of me. Everyone else of importance in my life knew me and was aware of the big part Hayley played in my life. David was relatively new into my life and had no sense of the history I had with Hayley. I am the first to accept that my attachment to her is most out of the ordinary and so I can't blame David for not understanding and for seeing my 'Hayley collection' as just being a teenage crush that should now be long outdated. My mistake was in not being assertive and claiming who I really was, but that is directly related to one's sense of self-worth and I was still too dependent on people's approval. But this devastation, which my lack of self-worth had led me to, set me on the path towards my next lesson.

> ***Always believe in your self-worth so
> you can communicate with confidence,
> without being fearful of reprisals.***

Six months after we were married we moved to Perth so that David could take up the appointment of Director of Music at the

Cathedral. Here in Perth David and I took our Profession vows in the Franciscan Third Order. This is the Anglican equivalent of the Roman Catholic 'Secular Franciscans'. There are three Orders: The First Order is the Brothers of St. Francis who live a monastic life but also go out and help in the wider community; the Second Order is the Sisters of St. Clare, known as the Poor Clares, who live a contemplative life within the walls of their convent; the Third Order are people who live their normal lives out in the world but who live according to the values set out by St Francis.

It was against this devout religious backdrop that, in 1981, I heard that Hayley was coming to Australia to be a guest on Michael Parkinson's talk show. When I heard this advertised, I was filled with an excitement and an anticipation that I can only liken to a child just before Christmas. It was then that I realized it coincided with a dinner engagement at the home of a friend, who was a priest and colleague from the Cathedral. Having gone through all sorts of excuses in my mind that I could give for getting out of the dinner commitment, I decided there was only one thing to do—to be honest and explain that this was really important to me, and, at the risk of appearing to have no manners at all, state that I would have to watch it and hold my dinner until it was over. What gall!

This determination had been born from my continuous regret of parting with the contents of my school case. It was too late to cancel the dinner appointment, so acting quite out of character, and with David totally disgusted with me, we arrived at the door: David with wine in hand; me with audio cassette recorder in hand. I announced the predicament I was in and felt such relief when our host enthusiastically said, "Hayley Mills!

Oh, I think she's gorgeous! Yes, we'll put dinner on hold while we watch it. I'd love to see her too!" I was grateful that I had spoken up and not had to learn this lesson the hard way.

Always ask for what you want.

His accommodating wife very kindly altered dinner to a later time, now having to try to keep dinner warm for an hour without ruining it for us. I recorded the interview, hanging on Hayley's every word, for I had no idea what was happening in her life at this point, either personally or professionally. The media didn't seem to touch on her out here in Australia anymore. I discovered that was because she was now involved with working in theatre in England rather than much in the way of films. I was flooded with excitement as I experienced the sense of having her presence in my life again. I had only a couple of photos of her now—the one which had been framed in my room at the time of relinquishing the collection four years earlier, and a recent one from the newspaper when she had arrived in Australia for this appearance on 'Parkinson'. I listened to the tape of the interview so many times over the years that it is surprising it didn't wear out. I was so elated to have this link, once more, with my beloved Hayley.

In 1985 we acquired a video recorder and I thereby started my new 'Hayley collection'—this time of her films on video. I stopped at nothing to get copies of her films. It was around this time that an aunt gave to me an article from a 1981 English Woman's Day magazine that she had stumbled on entitled 'Hayley Mills' Dream Home'. This gave me a mysterious sense of being part of her life—having an insight into her personal life. In the article Hayley was quoted as saying that she enjoyed inviting friends to her home for lunch on Sundays. I had a strong longing to be a part of that scene; I felt that I should be a friend in her home, after all no one loved her like I did, nor missed her like I did! *How ridiculous you sound, Helen—you've never even met her!*

I often wondered what it would be like to be a friend in her home, imagining what it would *feel* like to be sitting on her lounge, chatting, with a cup of tea in hand, and laughing and sharing as friends. If anyone had been able to read my mind they would have thought me fanciful at best and pitiful at worst.

I continued collecting on video any movie of Hayley's that came into my reach. As I was not living in Sydney, my mum was responsible for checking the Sydney TV programme each week for any of Hayley's films. I had given her a list of known films that I hadn't yet been able to see. One evening, while visiting David's mother in Sydney, I noticed in the TV programme a movie listed for 3 am starring Hayley—'What Changed Charlie Farthing'. I had never heard of that movie, and wondered why it was that my mother had overlooked it, so I phoned her and asked about it. In her programme Hayley's name did not appear, nor was the movie title on my list of Hayley's films not yet seen, so how could she have known? However, Mum set her video recorder on 'timer' to automatically video it for me. Unfortunately the channel's programming had been running late, so we managed to have the last half of the preceding movie and the first half of Hayley's. I kept it nonetheless and patiently waited until an opportunity presented itself to see it again (which did ultimately come, years later).

Having a growing collection of Hayley's movies was wonderful, but they didn't replace the *personal* photos of Hayley that I had forfeited. The photos from her films, which had been in my treasured collection, I was actually replacing on the videos, but nothing of her personal life was being revealed to me, and I really missed that. All through the years I had yearned to have those photos back—how I missed them . . . how I missed her! That sounds so silly, I know, but I knew the reality of that feeling. I was so pleased when my mother's next-door neighbour returned from an overseas trip with a photo, taken especially for me, of Hayley's pavement square outside Grauman's Chinese Theatre in Hollywood where she'd had her hand and footprints, along with her autograph, imprinted into the pavement on 22nd February, 1964 [photo 7]. I hadn't asked for the photo, but my attachment to Hayley was still well known.

Meanwhile, in 1985, David and I had moved from Perth back to the East Coast so that he could attend Theological College. It was there that we met another student, named Geoff, who lived with his wife and two young sons in the flat beneath ours. David and I became good friends with Geoff and his family, but it was Geoff and I who developed a strong friendship together—we understood each other in a profound way. We confided in each other that we were in emotionally empty marriages and we found that we were both trying to engender a loving response from our partners, neither of whom seemed interested. We both sought a foundation of deep mutual love on which to build our marriages, but neither of us felt we had that. Wanting to see each other's heart's desire met, we even tried to speak with the other's spouse to help in this regard, but our efforts went unheeded.

After almost two years of this close friendship, it caused great consternation to both of us to realize that we had come to recognise in each other the love of our lives. I had dreamed of having a husband who was my soul mate who would treasure and value my essence, as I would his, and who would understand love as I understood it, but I didn't have that in my marriage, and therefore never expected to find it. When such a soul mate appeared it created chaos. If it were not bad enough that we were both married, *it was not acceptable to fall in love with the **wrong** person at Theological College!* This was an impossible situation. I could no longer stay living at the College, so I was giving thought to the idea of testing my vocation with the Poor Clares nearby at Stroud. This seemed extreme perhaps, but I was facing a rather insurmountable problem, I thought. However, discovering (after eleven years of wanting children) that I now was pregnant only added to my dilemma. Too late to think of joining the Poor Clares! So, I moved out and stayed with my eldest sister, Leonie (with whom I had a very close friendship), on her farm at Gloucester.

On 3rd October 1987, I gave birth to my darling daughter. I was in a room with three other ladies, all of whom had given birth to girls. Two of them were naming their daughters Hayley, and I was naming my daughter Gemma Rose. 'Gemma' because she was so precious, my treasure, my gem, and 'Rose' because it is the symbol of love, along with being one of Hayley's names (Hayley Catherine Rose Vivien). Of all people, you'd expect that *I* would have been the one to call my daughter Hayley, but to have to go through the remainder of my days needing to refer to Hayley as Hayley Mills, to differentiate her from my daughter, was too impersonal, too absurd.

I fell so much in love with Gemma that my life should have been complete. The mother in me was filled to the brim and over-flowing with love and fulfilment. But the wife in me pined for the love of my life, and then there was that void that only Hayley could fill. *Now how could there be a void within me when I had never met that person to start with?* Ah, but I *knew* her. She was a real part of me somehow—she was within the chambers of my heart.

1) The Le Mesurier family 1957 (aged 8).

2) The family again in 1962 (aged 13).

3) Mum and Dad (Edith and Bert) 1979.

4) Three sisters. From left: Elaine, me and Leonie 1999.

5) Twin Cousins, (left to right) me and Beth, aged 3.

6) Twin Cousins, (left to right) Beth and me, aged 11.

7) Hayley's autograph in the pavement outside
Grauman's Chinese Restaurant.

PART TWO

They Said
I Couldn't Do It

One day in April 1991, having walked into the house laden with full shopping bags, I stooped as I passed the TV and pulled the knob to turn it on. To relieve my aching arms I headed for the kitchen, dumping the bags on the floor. As I did this I heard Ray Martin say that tomorrow one of his guests on 'The Midday Show' would be "former Disney child-star Hayley Mills". Can you imagine my excitement when I heard him say her name? What if I had been two minutes later into the house? What if I hadn't turned the TV on as I passed it? What if I had put the shopping bags down in the kitchen first and then come back to turn the TV on? I wouldn't have even known she was in Australia! Was this just chance? *I didn't think so.* I did spiritual cartwheels and ran around the room exclaiming, "Hayley, my beloved Hayley!"

It was then that the reality of the possibility of seeing her in person came to me. Up until now there had only ever been one previous time when I'd had a slight thought of hopefully seeing her in person. That had been ten years earlier in late April 1981 when David and I were in London for him to sit exams at the Royal College of Organists. We were walking around the West End of London on a Sunday afternoon and I gazed at the billings of the theatres as we passed in the hope of seeing her name or photo, but as David had no interest, I knew better than to try to pursue a search for her. We were in London for him, not for me. Other than for that one time, the idea of ever seeing

Hayley one day in the flesh had never entered my head as that just seemed so far fetched—such fantasy.

However, now she was to be in *Sydney*. When she had been in Australia in 1981 for 'Parkinson' she was on the east coast, whereas I was in Perth on the west coast, but she was now to be in Sydney and I was only a ninety-minute drive away! I ran to the phone and rang 'The Midday Show' at Channel Nine to acquire a seat in the audience, but they were booked out and weren't interested in trying to assist me. I was told abruptly that there was a bus company that organized to bring people to be the audience for the show, and that it was fully booked. The lady on the other end of the phone was dismissive of me, so I hung up feeling angry. She hadn't understood how important this was to me, but I was in no position to argue.

When David came home from work, I told him of my attempt to be in the audience of 'The Midday Show'. With a screwed up face displaying complete disapproval, he said, "You what?!" He was not very tolerant of things like this, as he couldn't comprehend why anyone would act in a manner that he wouldn't. Believing that he saw me as quite ridiculous, I realized how little he actually knew me: how little he was actually interested in me. So I resolved that I would do whatever I needed to, where Hayley was concerned, and not allow his opinion to influence me. Here were definite signs of my growth; my assertiveness was emerging! It came from my suppressed anger over many years, and now here I was, again with an issue relating to Hayley, which was something far too important to me to let David put a stop to. I had learnt from my past mistake. I was angry, more so with *myself* than with David, for having allowed him, fourteen years earlier, to intimidate and manipulate me into parting with my treasured 'Hayley collection'. How I had missed it, how I had missed her, and how I still yearned for her presence in my life. Her place in my heart had never wavered.

Never give your power away to another.

I had now resolved that never again would I give my power away. It had been a hard lesson to learn and had cost me dearly, but I wasn't forfeiting or relinquishing anything of Hayley, nor of myself, again. I set up a video in preparation to record Hayley as I watched 'The Midday Show' the next day. It was now ten years since seeing her on 'Parkinson' and it felt to me as if I were about to see my dearest friend again after a ten-year absence. As soon as I saw her appear on the screen I was completely overwhelmed with emotion and I began sobbing. This was *my Hayley*—oh, I knew her so well!

This unexpected emotional outburst took me so completely by surprise. *What was this about?* I didn't understand why I reacted so passionately. I was *stunned* by my reaction. *What was in the depths of my soul to cause this?*

Once I had ascertained from her interview that she was in Australia to tour with the show 'The King and I', and would be performing in Sydney later in the year, I had something to look forward to and was able to plan to buy tickets for her show. She was, however, touring Australia with this production and I had four months to wait until its Sydney season was to begin. I eagerly watched for the opening date for bookings and pounced immediately to obtain two great seats for Monday 28th October. Monday was David's one day off a week, and this was to be an outing to celebrate my forty-second birthday, which would have taken place three days earlier. I didn't ask him if I could book the tickets, I just did it. By asking I would have been giving him the power to say no, and I was not going to give him that power. I was asserting my power over this very important issue. However, I didn't know at the time just how eventful those ensuing four months would be, with my marriage splitting up for a third and final time in September. So by the time 28th October came around it was my mother who came with me to see the show.

Mum was very pleased that this opportunity for me to see Hayley on stage had presented itself after such a very difficult and trying period in my life.

It was a precious time for Mum and me, as we very rarely had the opportunity of doing something special like this together. Furthermore, it was an enormous thrill for her to be going to see Hayley—after all, I had made Hayley a house-hold name in my family.

With Gemma's baby-sitting arrangements in place, the evening started with Mum and me catching a bus from her home on the lower north shore of Sydney into the city, enjoying a meal together, followed by the double delight of seeing a spectacular show *and* seeing Hayley *live*. It was a wonderful experience to share with my mother, and it was exciting to be enjoying this adventure together. As Hayley made her entrance onto the stage, and 'Anna' appeared before us, I impulsively burst into applause. It was solo applause for a few embarrassing seconds and then the whole audience accompanied me with their applause. Although the show, in all it's spectacular Siamese colour, unfolded in front of me, I spent the whole evening with my eyes firmly-set just on

Hayley, soaking up her presence before me. We had wonderful seats—I was able to see her face quite clearly and all of her facial expressions. What a delight! What a dream come true!

It was, however, most surprising when, upon the curtain closing on Hayley, I once again found myself sobbing. I was paralysed with tears. We were the very last to leave the theatre that evening. I was trying to stop my sobbing before venturing out in the street to face the world again. I could see that the ushers were looking at me wondering what my problem was. I later realized that my emotion that evening stemmed from the finality of three things. The curtain had closed all right, but not only on Hayley. The curtain had also closed on my fifteen-year marriage and on any future with Geoff (as news had reached me that he had remarried during the time that I was working through my marriage with David—but that's another story!)... three endings to three of the most profound relationships in my life. The emotion engendered in me from the curtain closing on my time with Hayley had served as the catalyst for releasing all this other suppressed emotion. I had released the emotional beach balls that I had been holding down under the surface, and out it all came with surprising force.

However, with endings come new beginnings. Little did I know what was in store for me in ways of new beginnings! Eileen Caddy wrote: "Expect the most wonderful things to happen in your life, not in the future, but right now". I had often affirmed this, but, with the endings that I had experienced, it was difficult to see it working in my life. Nonetheless, I continued to affirm it, along with other affirmations, to attract wonderful adventures and happy experiences into my life. In hindsight it is evident that it did work!

In the taxi on our way home from the theatre, my mother, in her attempt to comfort me, told me how fortunate I had been to see Hayley in person on stage, and from such wonderfully positioned seating, but that I now must have a grateful heart and not dwell on hankering to see Hayley again. The tickets, after all, were expensive for me—not something I could repeat easily.

'Brilliant! Yes! See her again!' my inner voice urged. How could I now *not* dwell on wanting to see her again? I had been in almost touching distance of her (given several rows and an orchestra pit!). This was no ordinary famous celebrity—this was my beloved Hayley, my dearest friend from thirty years back! Had my mother understood nothing? She had a better understanding than anybody else did, and yet, did she too, not get it? So, with my new resolve firmly in place, I began brainstorming on how I could get to see her again.

In our youth, Beth and I had been regular visitors to the stage door of the Tivoli theatre in Sydney. Beth had a deep admiration for June Bronhill, and, as we both loved 'The Sound of Music', over time we attended fourteen matinees, sitting in the cheap seats way up in the 'gods' of the theatre. So we were no novices to stage doors. June Bronhill, who played Maria, had become quite accustomed to us, often saying, "You two girls here again?" Also, Beth and I had both been involved in amateur theatre ourselves: Beth with straight theatre and me with musical theatre. So it seemed only natural to ask Beth to accompany me to a matinee of 'The King and I' and to come to the stage door with me after the show.

It was with great excitement that, on 8th November, Beth and I eagerly waited outside the stage door after having attended the matinee. We waited, and we waited. One other man was doing the same and we chatted with him. I am sure all the cast must have filed past us before a lady came out and asked us: "Are you waiting to see Miss Mills?" We eagerly replied that we were, but she then said, "Miss Mills has asked me to tell you that she won't be coming out in between shows today." Beth quickly explained that I had come from Newcastle and that it was so important to me. Beth had come a similar distance from the Blue Mountains, but that didn't get mentioned as she was focused on me, and how important it was for *me* to see Hayley.

My only opportunity was after a matinee. I wasn't going to put myself at risk by being out in the city, alone, until near midnight waiting for the evening performance to end, and then have to face the dangers of public transport at that time of the morning. I might have been more likely to take risks had I not had a little daughter who was so precious to me and who relied on me, but, as it was I couldn't jeopardize my safety like that, not even for my dream of meeting Hayley.

The lady apologized, but said there was nothing she could do. She seemed such a lovely person and I felt such good vibes from her. She didn't make me feel silly for being so disappointed. The other chap left, disappointed, but I found it too hard to pull myself away from where I knew Hayley to be. Seeing my disappointment the lady offered to take my programme and have Hayley autograph it, and then mail it back to me. She said that she already had a pile to be autographed and so mine could go with them. As I was giving her my address she interjected, "Just a minute—I can't promise anything, but I'll see if there's any chance of her autographing it while you wait." She took my programme and Beth and I waited.

After what must have been ten minutes, she returned to the stage door asking, quickly, for my name. I told her "Helen", and she crossed her fingers for me, and disappeared again. Five minutes later she re-appeared with a cheesy grin across her face and an autographed programme in hand which read 'For Helen, With Love Hayley Mills'. I thanked her warmly. Then, pulling myself away from the door that separated me from Hayley, set off with Beth.

We marvelled at what a lovely lady she was and how lovely it had been to have some interaction with her. I was so pleased to have Hayley's full-page portrait autographed, and also felt privileged for having met the lady at the stage door—she was so lovely. The thought crossed my mind that maybe if I had met Hayley I may have been disappointed, but this other lady had certainly put colour into my day. *This thought was only to dispel my disappointment and I knew deep down that it was only that.* It was with a grateful heart that I set off home, giving thanks for the blessings I had received. I framed the autographed portrait and it still hangs in my home today.

It didn't take long for the desire to meet Hayley to surface again. My logic had settled me, the day at the stage door, but the intuitive side didn't rest. It was now the 7th December and I realised that if I didn't act soon I would miss all opportunity to meet her, as she was due to leave Sydney within a few weeks. Gemma was watching Hayley's film 'The Trouble With Angels' when I had a 'scathingly brilliant idea'. As it was a Saturday, there would be a matinee performance today. I rang the theatre and asked, "If I were to come to the stage door today, in between performances, would I get to see Hayley? Would she actually come out in between performances today?"

The person on the other end of the phone enquired for me and brought me the answer: "No."

So I asked, "How can I get to meet her?"

The girl on the other end of the phone had no idea so she put me onto someone else, who said that I *couldn't* get to meet her. I would not accept that! I asked to speak with someone else. This next person assured me that there was no way I could get to meet her. I asked to speak with someone else. This next person listened to my plight, but then launched into a verbal flourish explaining to me the celebrity status of Miss Mills, and how she couldn't be exposed to fans in this way. I explained that fans *were* meeting her. I had read in the paper that fans had met her at some charity function. Where could I get to know of such functions? Realizing that he wasn't going to convince me, he transferred me to the 'front of house'.

Once again I went through all the preamble explaining that I wanted to meet Hayley, and why, but this time I was given, "I work here and I haven't met her!" To which I retorted, "Then it's not that important to you!" I asked to speak with someone else. She transferred me to the Stage door—to guess whom—yes, the lovely lady with whom I'd had dealings on 8th November. Not realizing to whom I was speaking, I once more entered into my spiel of my plight, only this time this lady actually tried to do something to help.

"Are you the lady from Newcastle?" she asked. She actually remembered me and recognized my voice! "This must be very important to you—you're very persistent."

I said, "You don't know the half of it! You are the sixth person I have said all this to on this one phone call."

Although she could promise nothing, as my request was quite unprecedented, she assured me that she would speak with Miss Mills' dresser after the matinee, and that she'd phone me back that evening from her home, as she was unable to call long-distance from the stage door. I said I didn't need her to go to any personal expense, and that if she gave me a time I could phone her back. So we arranged for me to phone back in five hours (at 5.30 pm), and if she hadn't been able to ascertain anything by then we'd make another time for me to phone later. I set an alarm.

On the dot of 5.30 pm I phoned back and was greeted with, "Well, it's your lucky day! Miss Mills would be delighted to meet with you and your daughter!"

Persist: Never give up on your dream

For the appointment I was given the choice of any afternoon straight after the matinee, which ran Wednesdays and Saturdays. The following Saturday was suggested. I asked, "What's wrong with this coming Wednesday? I couldn't live with myself for a whole week!"

So the appointment was made for four days hence at 4.05 pm on 11th December. Bursting with excitement, I rang my mother (who was almost as thrilled for me as I was for myself), my sister Leonie (who was in awe of my boldness and success in such a quest), and my closest friends, whom I knew would be thrilled for me. There was another person whom I chose *not* to call since I knew her reaction would put a dampener on my excitement, as she was on an entirely different wavelength to me—my much-loved other sister, Elaine. Besides interpreting me as being juvenile over Hayley, she was a scientist and mathematician who saw things in black and white. She didn't have time for things that couldn't be explained by logic.

The next four days were spent in a state of disbelief. I kept thinking I'd wake up and find it was all a dream. I kept pinching myself to be assured that I was awake. What to wear? What about Gemma? What would I dress her in? She had her pre-school Christmas party that very day, which I could not expect her to miss, and then a two hour train journey—what state would she be in by the time she got to meet Hayley? She'd need a clean outfit to change into once we arrived at the theatre. I'd need to freshen up my make-up so I needed to remember to take some with me. I needed to make a list! So much activity and excitement going through my mind and body! What did I want to say to her? How would I appear to her? Like a raving lunatic? I almost felt like one! My mind never stopped. I couldn't sleep because of the mental activity and the nervous energy from my excitement.

Thirty years attachment, dedication, obsession, love—call it what you will—and I was now actually on my way to meet her! I collected Gemma from her pre-school Christmas party, full of excitement for what was ahead. On the train trip down to Sydney I was overcome with awe and wonder at the reality that I was actually travelling to meet with Hayley! What would transpire? Would it be a brief meeting in the reception area? Would it be an exchange of pleasantries? Would we get taken back-stage somewhere to meet her? Her dressing room, perhaps? Would it be of two minutes duration, or ten, or fifteen? What would I say to her? Would Gemma give me some space and peace or would she be demanding and frustrating? She could ruin the whole moment for me! I prayed for a quietened mind, and a right outcome. I tried reading the book I had brought with me for the train trip but couldn't concentrate on it so I sat meditating and felt the peace of knowing I was okay and that everything would resolve in the way it should—however that was.

The rain was pouring down as the train drew to a halt at the platform at Central Station. What terrible weather for us to have to contend with. Still, I couldn't let some rain ruin *this* day. We were soaked by the time we arrived at the theatre. The performance was still underway, so we were able to get to the 'ladies' room easily, without lots of other people around, and freshen ourselves up, although there was not much I could do about our soaked feet. Then, by the influx of women streaming in, I knew that the show was over. We emerged into the throng of patrons mingling in the foyer. Some, no doubt, were waiting for the heavy rain to ease before venturing outside. I wasn't wasting time by waiting for lighter rain: I opened my umbrella, scooped Gemma up on my hip, and ran for my life from the theatre, out and around the corner, to the stage door.

I had been warned what to expect by the lady at the stage door (whose name I now knew to be Diane). She had explained that I would be confronted at the stage door and unless I made it clear that I had an appointment, and that Miss Mills was expecting me, I would be turned out within seconds. So it was with bravery that, at 4 pm on Wednesday 11th December 1991, we knocked at the stage door and barged in to avoid being drenched further by the pouring rain.

Diane certainly knew what she was talking about! We were met with a chorus of "You can't come in here!" from several very convincing characters who were gathering to block our further progress. Just as I was about to defend our entry, a hidden voice called out "Are you Helen?" Once I had answered yes, the 'hound dogs' were called off. Diane asked us to take a seat while she let Hayley's dresser know we were there. What was about to happen, I wondered? *This* is the moment of all moments fast approaching. Catherine, the dresser, appeared and came over to talk with us. She said that Hayley was on the phone but shouldn't be long. She was very friendly and enquired with interest as to where my desire to meet Hayley came from. I gave her a five-minute summary of the last thirty years. She was amazed and impressed with my consistent sense of commitment to Hayley throughout the years.

Then she went to see if Hayley was off the phone. On her return she beckoned us to follow her. Would we actually get to meet her in her dressing room? *Yes!* We approached the door— the last down the long corridor—and as we looked through it **there she was!** There stood my long-lost dearest friend. She walked over to us. Oh yes, it was her all right—so natural, so warm, so welcoming, so *her!* My instinct was to rush at her with a big hug, but decorum knew its place. While emotions were creating wonderment for me, Catherine introduced Gemma to Hayley, and Hayley crouched down to talk with her. Gemma hugged Hayley, which was reciprocated. I heard Gemma say to Hayley, "I've loved you all my life." I know I was listening to what followed but there was so much going through me at the time that I only remember what I *saw* before me and that was Hayley being so delightful to my awestruck daughter.

After a minute or so (or was it a life-time?) Hayley stood up, faced me, and as Catherine introduced us, Hayley looked at me with such warmth that I instinctively outstretched my arms to her and asked, "May I?"

She responded, "Of course!"

And there we were embracing! To have done anything else would have seemed so awkward and unnatural. As we released our hug I said to her, "Oh, Hayley, we've been friends for thirty years, you just haven't known about it."

She beamed as she said, "What a lovely thing to say!"

"I have followed your life and career very closely and feel that I know you so well," I explained.

She invited us into her dressing room, as, up until now, we had been standing in the doorway. I handed her the gift of an opal necklace and as I did I said, "Here is a little gift from us, something to remind you of your time in Australia."

"For me? How thoughtful," she replied. She read the little card attached first, and exclaimed, "Le Mesurier? Have you heard of the actor John Le Mesurier?"

As I nodded yes I said, "We think he's a distant relative. The likeness between him and my father's family is uncanny!"

"I've never heard of anyone other than for John with that surname."

"It's my maiden name," I quickly added.

She questioned, "Your maiden name?"

"Yes, my marriage broke up about eight weeks ago. I had given my married name when making the appointment to meet you, but I am now reclaiming my maiden name."

I told her that my mother had come with me to see the show on 28th October. I explained that she had seen me through the thirty years of my attachment to Hayley and that she supported me with it in contrast to the way David had belittled me over it. Hayley said she was sorry that I had such turmoil in my life.

"What a hard time for you!"

"No, it's all right," I said.

By this time she had opened the gift and said, "Oh it's just lovely! It really is lovely. I'll put it on right now. You shouldn't be spending your money on me!"

I explained how I had always spent my money on her, buying the movie magazines that had photos and articles about her. I had not only *read* all the articles I had of her, but that I had *studied* them. She looked at me in astonishment. I told her of how I had discarded all the photos and articles of her because I was told to, and how I had had to live with my stupidity ever since and also had to live without them, which was like having lost her. She looked at me with such intensity. Her eyes became moistened as she listened to me and she gave a sigh—she understood my pain and sense of loss.

She offered me a wine, which I accepted, only to find that she wasn't having one with me, as she wouldn't drink in between shows. I should have realized that and declined, but it was too late, the wine was being poured.

Hayley then took Gemma by the hand and led her to a large wardrobe. In it were the dresses she wore in the show. She pushed them apart to show them to us. Big-skirted dresses with heavy metal hoops on the hemline—what a weight for her to carry around on stage, and to dance in! No wonder she was slim! Gem was so cute as she looked at Hayley and soaked her up. She really was in awe of Hayley. Perhaps she was trying to relate her to Pollyanna, or another of Hayley's characters. Whatever it was she was thinking, she was mesmerized by Hayley. This resulted in her being very quiet and allowed me to be present in the moment of this special time with Hayley.

As Hayley and I enjoyed conversation together, we exchanged comments on our failed relationships and discussed the higher aspects of our experiences. She thought that a particular book, which she was reading, would benefit me with where I was at in my life. She said that when she was finished reading it she would happily pass it on to me. As she started telling me of the author, I leant and picked the very book out of my bag and held it up. We were reading the same book at the same time! How crazy was that? It was 'The Road Less Travelled', by M. Scott Peck.

I asked her about the book that she had co-edited entitled 'My God'. It was mentioned in the programme of 'The King and I' but I had searched for it and couldn't locate it. She said, "No, you won't find it as it's now out of print, but I can get you one and I will send it to you." Wow! That meant that there would be further contact. Today would not be the end. Yet, even if it were to be so, my dream would have been realized.

Three quarters of an hour flew by and I knew that if I didn't leave within a few minutes I ran the risk of being asked to leave, as Hayley obviously needed rest between shows. After Hayley had written down my address (to post her book to) I brought my time with her to an end. Hayley acknowledged that she not only needed some rest but also needed to write a few Christmas cards. As we were about to depart Hayley thought that we should have some photos taken together so rushed out to ask Catherine if there was a camera handy. She was unable to locate one, but *luckily* I was able to produce a little one out of my handbag and so Catherine took some photos of us together [photos 8-11]. I was so thrilled to think I had in my possession photos of Hayley taken with us.

As we hugged goodbye at the door, Hayley said to me, "When you arrived you said that we had been friends for thirty years but I just didn't know about it. Well, I feel I do. We are kindred spirits." Reeling with delight at her words, I felt tears forming in my eyes, only to notice that the same was happening for her. *Quickly, pinch me, for I must be in a dream*! Hayley added, "Don't be sad that you lost all the photos of me, because maybe you had to lose *them* in order to find *me*." *'Find me'! She acknowledges that I have found her! I will make sure that I never lose her again.*

We embraced, enjoying a lingering hug. The look we gave each other told of the warmth between us. Hayley then crouched down to Gemma and hugged her too. She was so beautiful with Gemma. I will always remember how sweet she was to her. Leaving the theatre, I left behind one of the most exciting experiences of my life.

As we trained home, I was in another space altogether. I thanked Gem for being so well behaved and being such a delight. I praised her several times during the trip, as I really was so impressed with her. She had allowed my time with Hayley to be so focused, and I was so appreciative of that. It was as though Gemma had, at a spiritual level, sensed how important this was for me and had honoured it. Of course, she knew it was important, but she was only four and not able to process it in the way that it transpired. She has proven many times over in her life that she is an old soul with the wisdom that she carries beyond her years.

That evening I phoned both my mother and my sister, Leonie, to relate my excitement at the outcome of the day. They were so in awe of our adventure.

Several months later, Gemma and I were visiting my mother at the same time as my sister Elaine and her younger children were. Without thought, and with great enthusiasm, I told her about my meeting with Hayley and I asked her if she'd like to see the photos of the occasion, thinking she would at least humour me. With the same attitude that David had toward me (that I was childish), she dismissed me by saying, "No, I'm not interested, but my nine-year-old might be impressed by them." I was cut to the core by her attitude and stood frozen from the put-down. I was so close to tears but, needing to retain some dignity, I forced them back.

Later in the day when Elaine and children had left, Mum came to me and caringly said: "Don't let what Elaine said put a dampener on you where Hayley is concerned. This is a very special thing for you. Don't let someone else take that from you."

> **When knocked over, get up and brush**
> **yourself down.**
> **There will be others to uphold you.**

When I shared this experience with Leonie, she was very surprised. *She,* on the other hand, had been telling all her friends about my courage and boldness and how I had met with Hayley. She was proud of my achievement. She understood how much it meant to me.

8) and 9) Our first meeting, taken in Hayleys dressing room
at Her Majesty's Theatre, Sydney, 11th December, 1991.*

10) and 11) With a tired little Gemma 11th December, 1991.*

PART THREE

An Unlikely Prophecy

Weeks went by. My mother, sister and friends constantly enquired as to whether I had received the book from Hayley. Time and time again I had to say "no". I could feel their pity and scepticism of such a book ever arriving. They really didn't think my belief would be rewarded. But they hadn't felt the sincerity from Hayley that I had that day in her dressing room. I didn't doubt for a moment; I was only impatient to hear from her. Then one day I answered a knock at the door. The Australia Post courier handed me a parcel. It had been six weeks since Hayley had told me she would send the book, and true to her word, here it was. On the back of the parcel was written 'Sender: Ms H. Mills', and the address of her hotel in Melbourne. I felt so privileged to be given her hotel address.

Good things come to those who wait.

As I excitedly opened the parcel, I found, to my surprise, not only the book, but a chatty hand written letter from Hayley, within which she had given me her home address so we could keep in contact! I was struck with awe at her response to me. This was beyond anything I could have ever imagined would develop from the boldness of my pursuit to meet her. I had only originally sought to speak with her at the stage door! From my boldness had come the unexpected *appointment* to meet *with* her, and now this. Goethe's words "Whatever you can do, or dream you can, begin it now. Boldness has genius, power and magic in it" rang so true for me now, proving to me that my actions had started a chain of events—something I could never have imagined.

I wrote to Hayley at the hotel in Melbourne, thanking her for the book and her lovely letter, and expressing how honoured I was that she trusted me with her home address. She was showing me real friendship, not that of a celebrity to a fan. *I knew I was a real friend, but I really didn't expect her to feel that towards me. But she did.*

The book was fascinating. It was a compilation of comments given by many and varied high-profile people in answer to two questions that Hayley and her co-editor had posed to them: 'Who or what is your personal concept of God?' and 'What do you believe happens to you when you die?' I read through this book, captivated by what others had to say. There were religious leaders, film stars, politicians, comedians, singers, all sorts of people, some giving long explanations, others one short sentence. It was a brilliant idea for a book!

While deep in thought one day, it occurred to me that Hayley's ten month tour of Australia with 'The King and I' was rapidly coming to an end and that if I was to ever see her again my last chance to do so would be by going to Melbourne . . . *I could go for the final night of the show!* Where did that thought come from? It was as if someone else put the idea into my head. What a 'scathingly brilliant idea'! Having had final nights of my own I knew how exciting they were. *Yes*—I would train down to Melbourne for her final night and, hopefully, say hello again at the stage door as she left the theatre. So I phoned the theatre to find out if there were any seats still available for the final night on 15th February. I was told, "No, we're sold out." (Should have been expected, I guess). In my disappointment I asked, "Not even one?" To my surprise I was told, "Well, yes, there is *one*, but nobody wants just *one*." I joyfully retorted, "*I* do!" So, not caring where it was positioned in the theatre, I said I'd take it. I would've sat behind a column with my view totally obscured or stood up for the entire performance if necessary just to be there.

I booked accommodation with the YWCA back-packers hostel, as that was the only way I could afford the expenses of such a trip. Having done this, I rang Mum and Leonie to tell them of my endeavours. Suitably excited, they offered to assist with my expenses. Then I penned a letter to Hayley telling her of my intentions. I explained that I was coming down solely to see her in the final night of the show and in the hope that I may get to say hello to her again afterwards. I also said that I'd bring with me copies of the photos we'd had taken together in Sydney and that if I couldn't get to see her that I would leave them with Diane's counterpart at the stage door.

Having posted that letter to the hotel where she was staying, I realized that I still had to have Gemma looked after for the duration of my time away. So I asked David if he could manage to have her stay with him, knowing that he was very busy with his parish work, but he said he would be delighted to have her stay. Having explained why I was asking, he said to me in all seriousness, "Hayley's likely to invite you to the end of show party." I was shocked that he would say such a fanciful thing to me—it was strange coming from David. His attitude had certainly changed! Now here he was actually encouraging me in my love of Hayley, but with something so extreme, potentially feeding me hope for something that was definitely not going to happen. A "good for you, I hope you get to see her at the stage door" would have been more appreciated.

I scoffed at him and said sarcastically, "Thanks for that! As if!" I was just hopeful of actually seeing her personally—to hand her the photos, and to exchange a hug! To hope for more than that was unrealistic, and I didn't appreciate such an idea being put before me as a serious possibility.

Being on the over-night train to Melbourne had an excitement about it. I assumed, because passengers would be sleeping side-by-side, that I would be given a seat along-side another female for such a trip, but no, I found myself next to a nice-looking man about my own age. Although I found this awkward, he turned out to be very pleasant, and we chatted as the train rollicked along the track.

As we talked, time wore on and it soon was time to settle for the night. I had brought with me a rug and pillow. He had not. Suddenly I felt very uncomfortable at bringing out these things without offering him to share them, as the air-conditioning on the train was chilly. How self-conscious I was feeling! Because of this, there was no way I could put my head down to sleep. So, we talked *all* night rather than entering into a scenario that was too uncomfortable for me. By the time we arrived in Melbourne he was showing quite an interest in me, and asked for my phone number so he could phone me when we were both back in NSW. Not knowing how to say no politely, and not knowing if I wanted him to have it or not, and unable to think quickly, I gave it to him! He then offered for me to share his taxi and be dropped off prior to him as he was going further than me.

I considered that this would save me a taxi fare. That sounded good! So that's what I did.

As a result of this all-nighter with no sleep, I was intending to sleep during the day to catch up. However, this wasn't to be. Firstly, I arrived at 8am and couldn't get into the room until at least 10am. I filled in a little of the time by having my hair cut, as there was a hairdresser next door, but it was cut so short that I regretted having had it done. Looking good for tonight was so important to me and now here I was looking far from what I was happy with. A bad hair day doesn't do much for the self-esteem.

When I finally had the opportunity to sleep, there was so much noise around that it was impossible to do so. I decided to phone Hayley at the theatre to see if she had received my letter, only to be met by an unpleasant male voice on the other end of the phone thundering, "No, I *can't* put you through to Miss Mills! I can't put just *anyone* through to Miss Mills!" I explained that she would very likely accept my call, but no, he wasn't going to put me through to her. Absolutely astounded at his attitude, I hung up feeling totally deflated.

Later that afternoon, while travelling back on the tram after visiting a friend who lived in Melbourne, I experienced a thought that seemed to, yet again, come from without rather than from within—like a deep knowing given to me from an outside source, a knowing so intense that I was compelled to act upon it: *I should have asked to speak with Hayley's dresser rather than to her!*

So upon my return I did just that. Without hesitation this grumpy old man put me directly through. When the call was answered I explained who I was and before I could get the rest of my message out, Hayley's dresser exclaimed, "Helen, it's Catherine. I met you the day you came to meet Hayley in Sydney with your daughter." Oh, how delightful to have a friendly voice at the other end! So, Catherine was obviously travelling with Hayley as her dresser, not just assigned to her for Sydney. Catherine continued, "Hayley received your letter and I know that she wants to talk to you, but I don't know just where she is at this moment. Can you wait while I go in search of her?" Well, what's a girl to do? If Hayley *wants* to talk to me, then obviously I will wait! *Fancy, Hayley wanting to talk to **me**, not just me wanting to talk to her!*

Hayley came to the phone. "Helen!" she exclaimed. "How wonderful that you've come all this way just to see me! How was your trip down?" To save her the whole story I just said that I hadn't had any sleep. Next she asked if I needed a ticket as she could give me a house ticket. I thanked her but explained that I had already bought a ticket. Then she asked "Would you like to come backstage after the show and have a glass of champagne with me in my dressing room? I'll be having a short time with the producers first, and then we can get together."

What music to my ears! This was beyond what I had anticipated would be the outcome—this was a dream outcome for my journey. I thanked her and accepted the invitation, trying all the while to keep my composure. I said to her, "I'm so excited being here for your final night of the show".

"It's lovely for me that you've come all that way just to see me."

I replied, "No distance is too far."

"You're *very* sweet," Hayley added.

As I put the phone back on the hook, the enormous smile etched on my face attracted others to smile at me. So now, with great anticipation, I hurried off to get ready.

My hair was a great catastrophe, not only because it was so short, but because the entire natural blonde top layer had been cut off and my hair looked unusually dark. I didn't recognize the red-eyed reflection looking back at me from the mirror, but there it was staring back at me, so it must be me! I was so disappointed with the way I looked, but I put it into perspective—my looks weren't going to change in the next few hours, so there was nothing to be done except to stop looking in the mirror and be the person I *felt* inside and not be concerned about the appearance of the person I perceived in the mirror.

Beauty is in the eye of the beholder—not the mirror!

Once all ready, ticket in purse, door key in purse, lipstick in purse, tissue in purse and some money in purse (checklist complete), I ventured out into the street to catch a tram to the theatre.

This was not as straightforward as I had expected, as I had no idea which tram went past the theatre, or anywhere near it for that matter. I asked a passer-by but he, too, didn't know Melbourne at all. When a tram came I wanted to ask the driver or conductor, but one had to board the tram to do the latter—there was no access to the driver. Once on board I would feel foolish if it was not the tram I needed, and had to get off at the next stop to await another tram, or even worse if I was taken for a ride beyond the immediate area and couldn't get back in time. So, in the end I decided to set off on foot and walk to the theatre. Not a good idea in high-heeled shoes, but there you are—things you do when the end result is all that is important, and that was getting to the theatre on time. I couldn't feel my feet throbbing, as I was completely absorbed, focusing on what I was in Melbourne for and being present in each moment.

I was very lucky with my seat. It was in the dress circle, just to the right of the centre, and five rows up. Couldn't have asked for better, unless of course it was five rows from the orchestra pit, which is probably where I could've been sitting if I had accepted Hayley's offer of a house seat. But I was a 'happy little vegemite'. Seated next to me was a school principal who had a student from his school performing as one of the King's adorable children. We chatted and he introduced me to the child's mother, who, understandably, was so proud and excited.

The gong chimed and everyone was asked to take their seats. Within a few minutes, the maestro entered the orchestra pit, faced the applauding audience, bowed, turned to his attentively poised musicians, held up his baton, and, with a downward stroke, the overture burst forth with its magic. My heart was racing, caught up in the atmosphere in this theatre. I no longer felt anticipation, for I was in its midst. The curtain now up, I awaited Hayley's entrance from stage right. Keeping with my custom, upon her stepping into view I started with applause. Solo applause! Within moments all joined me, but I was definitely the instigator. Each time she entered or exited the stage I broke forth with applause and took the audience with me. I was excited!

At interval I remained in my seat. This proved interesting as I witnessed streamers being put on everyone's seat. So! This was going to have that exciting finish that I had anticipated. Again the gong sounded with the announcement for the patrons to take their seats for the second act. As people returned to their seats, and saw the streamers, there was buzzing in the air. By the end of the act the atmosphere in the theatre had become electrified with joyous appreciation, not only appreciation of this last performance, but of the whole ten months of the show's tour. Streamers were in flight; applause ecstatic; cheers deafening. The animated audience demanded curtain call after curtain call; my hands were red and hurting from clapping so enthusiastically, and occasionally I had to shake them to stop them tingling. Tears of emotion dropped from my cheeks onto my dress. These gentle tears were in vast contrast to the sobbing tears I had shed at the end of the show when I saw it for the first time in Sydney with my mother. This was not to be an ending in the same way as then—after all, I still had the glass of champagne with Hayley to look forward to in her dressing room.

How far my relationship with Hayley had developed since meeting her on that wet December day, just two months ago. As the crowd made its way to the exits, I grinned with delight knowing that *I* was going to be privileged in a way they were not. This was not a smug 'I'm more important than you' feeling, but rather a sense of being so blessed.

I made my way to the stage door and to the desk of the grumpy old man. I stated my case that Hayley was expecting me and could he please let her dresser know that Helen was at the desk. Without a quip he picked up the phone and, with a movement of his head, gestured for me to go through the closed door. As I did, the crowds who were waiting to collect their children from the dressing rooms strained their necks to see down the corridor. Their eyes were on me as I entered the 'no-go' area. How they must have wanted to go through to their children and see the back-stage environment. I have to admit, I felt very honoured being allowed through the door into the sacrosanct area. As I walked down the corridor, Catherine was walking toward me. She greeted me warmly and took me to a seat outside Hayley's dressing room. She explained that Hayley would come out after having time with the producers etc., who were all congregated with her in her dressing room. I said there was no problem as to how long Hayley may be, as at least she was going nowhere without coming out of the door in front of me. I couldn't have been happier—only a door away from Hayley!

I watched most of the cast file past me as they made their way out to the street, many still made-up. I smiled at them and, when I actually recognised someone for the part they had played, I spoke to them, congratulating them on a wonderful performance. A few of them stopped and chatted, which was really nice for me. The children were so sweet, some older ones having the younger ones by the hand, taking them out to their awaiting parents. Some of these littlies were so very young I was surprised that the parents weren't allowed, or even actually required, to be with them. The queue of performers leaving the theatre had virtually come to an end, and I was sitting, no longer with any activity to entertain me.

By this time it was well over an hour. Catherine had come back to me several times to apologise for Hayley's delay. Each time I assured her that I was perfectly happy waiting. I had no where else to be and no curfew so I wasn't at all concerned with how long Hayley was taking with her bosses; it was not only what was expected of her but also what I would have assumed would take place after the final show of a ten-month tour. There would be much to celebrate and discuss. No, I was content to sit, for I knew that at the end of my wait I would see Hayley.

After further time had elapsed, Catherine returned and said to me that she was so embarrassed that I had been left waiting for so very long. In order to help me cope with my disappointment, that she was determined I must be feeling, she told me something which she obviously had not wanted to tell me herself (she would have rather left it for Hayley to say) but, given the length of time that had passed, she took it upon herself to tell me not to be discouraged, because *Hayley was going to invite me to the end of show party!* In absolute disbelief at what I was hearing I exclaimed, "Pardon? Are you sure?"

"Oh yes," Catherine replied, "very sure. I'm sorry you heard it from me, but at least it gives you heart while you wait." *(How weird that David had said that this would happen! How could he have seen this possibility when it was so improbable?)* "I really hope she won't be much longer. It's difficult for her to just leave the celebration as it's taking place in *her dressing room."* I completely understood and assured her again that I was happy to wait, no matter how long it took.

Then the door opened, and out stepped a vision of loveliness.

"Helen, you've been so very patient. Thank you for waiting all this time. I am so sorry." As these words were being spoken, Hayley moved to me and embraced me so warmly that I was quite taken aback. That gesture in itself made my long train trip, the discomfort of trying to sleep beside the man, my resulting tiredness, the rudeness from the difficult man at the stage door, and even this long wait, worth it all. I complimented her on her performance and the success of the show, and asked how she was feeling now that the final curtain had closed. She reminisced at what a wonderful experience it had all been for her but that she was now more than ready to go home to her family in England. I detected that she was very tired from the constant drain that this ten-month tour had taken on her physically, mentally, and no doubt emotionally. "Do you have to rush off? I would very much like for you to be my guest at the party that is being put on for us upstairs." Well, it was all I could do to contain my excitement. After all I didn't want her to see me as being *too* eager. Calmly I asked, "Are you sure?"

"Quite sure!" she emphatically replied, and with that she beckoned to Catherine and we were on our way to the party.

We stood waiting for the lift and when the doors parted we were face to face with John Frost, the producer of the show. We stepped into the lift and Hayley introduced me to him.

"John, I'd like you to meet my friend Helen." *HER FRIEND!!!* She said I was *her friend!* Well, of course I was, but to hear that *she* thought of me as such, and for her to *say* so, was music to my ears—very unexpected music. After the exchange of pleasantries, Hayley delved into her dilly bag and brought out a small box of Royal Jelly vials, which she offered to all in the lift. I had no idea what it was, so I just put it in my bag. After I had the opportunity of finding out just what it was, and discovering that it was indeed very good for you, I ventured to try it. (I still have the empty vial in a box of keepsakes).

The doors of the lift opened revealing the party room. The sound of the music was so loud that I was surprised we hadn't heard it in the lift as we approached the floor. There were people everywhere. We took up residence at a large round table and I ended up sitting between Hayley and Walter Van Nieuwkuyk, the executive producer. On the other side of Hayley was seated John Frost. Also seated with us were producer Tim MacFarlane and director Christopher Renshaw. Other production personnel were also seated at the table. I wanted so much to take some photos of the evening but didn't want to appear pushy and obvious, so I asked Hayley if she would like me to take some photos of her with her friends from the show so that she had memories of the party. I explained that I had a camera in my bag which had a fresh film in it and that I would happily use it on taking photos for her. She seemed surprised and delighted with my offer, enquiring, "Would that not be asking too much of you?" "Of course not!" I assured her.

As the chatter progressed, Hayley eventually excused herself from the table and mingled. John moved into her seat so that he could talk with me. I think he felt I was a little out of my comfort zone, knowing no one except Hayley and now she had moved on and out into the party. I had been sitting watching Hayley as she interacted with others, quite in awe of her elegance. John was very nice. He made conversation with me, which I did appreciate. He asked me how I had met Hayley. I thought that was a bit tricky to answer as I didn't want to come across to him as an over-the-top fan, for I didn't see myself as that, but I couldn't have blamed others for seeing me as such. I made a comment, which showed me up in rather a bad light, and I could have allowed the floor boards to have opened and swallowed me if only I had been accepted by them, but even they weren't impressed. What I said was that I kept expecting Hayley to turn around and, finding me there again, think, "Oh no, not her again!" (This showed my insecurities). John retorted,

"Then you don't know Hayley very well, for she would never think such a thing."

And he was so right. Hayley was too enlightened a being for that. But wow, it showed that I wasn't. Hayley's whole aspect of life came from a platform of love. She was so different to the Hollywood images of screen stars. She was not besotted with herself, she wasn't concerned that a hair might be out of place, or that her lipstick needed retouching. She was not self-absorbed at all; she was others-absorbed. Even when one young man approached her, and began gushing over her, putting his arms around her, and invading her space, she graciously allowed him to be himself. She agreed to a photo with him, and then, with such charm, she smiled and just moved on to others, leaving him very happy with himself. Surely she must have felt uncomfortable about it and thought of him as I did! Inwardly, I was looking down on him and dismissing him as a distasteful ogre that Hayley surely would shudder from having lounging over her shoulders. Hayley not only didn't show any such impression, she even seemed accepting of this young man's tactile disposition, without encouraging it. Oh wow, was she showing me to myself. I had so much more still to learn about conscious awareness and love. She had such grace of spirit.

I continued to observe her as she mingled, laughed, hugged, and shed a few tears with her fellow thespians. I was delighted when she would beckon me to come over to where she was chatting—with a person or a small group of people—and ask me to take photos. I had just taken a snap of her with John Frost [photo 12] when he asked, "Have you two had a photo taken together tonight?" Hayley turned to me and, looking me straight in the eye, said, "No, we haven't!" He put his hand out for my camera, which I handed to him, and he snapped a lovely photo of us [photo 13]. (So I have an indelible memory of how unhappy I was with the way my hair looked that evening. However, because it is a photo of me with Hayley, a photo from which my memories of that evening reach out like tentacles, I cherish it).

At 2 am a male voice boomed over the loudspeaker system heralding the end of the party with the announcement: "Time please, ladies and gentlemen." The immediate mass exit amused me. We made our way to the lifts. Reluctant to leave her, I asked Hayley if there was anything I could help her with. She accepted my offer, suggesting I could help her clear out her things from her dressing room. As we did, she piled bouquets of beautiful flowers into my arms and said I could have them! I resisted by saying, "But Hayley, these have been given to you with such love from people who are very special to you."

"Yes," she said, "But I can't take them on the plane back to London with me." I managed to share them with some other folk who were there with us, and kept only two bouquets, one of which I gave back to Hayley and suggested she could enjoy it in her hotel room until she had to leave. So with all her goods piled up on a wardrobe trolley, we headed for the car park. With frivolity she jumped aboard the trolley that her understudy, Christine Mahoney, and Walter were wheeling along [photos 14-15].

The others departed, leaving Hayley and me to transfer the things into her car. As we did, she asked how I was going to get back to my accommodation. I said I'd go out to the street and hail a taxi. I hadn't given any thought, until then, as to how I would get back. It was a fearful thought that I would have to venture out to the street on my own, looking for a taxi. She exclaimed, "No, not at this time of night. I'll drop you off." With an exceptionally grateful heart, I accepted and got in to the awaiting Saab. I asked how it was that she had a car, as I had assumed she'd be using taxis to take her from hotel to theatre and back again. She said that Saab, being one of the sponsors of the show, had offered her the use of the car for as long as she needed it. She was very appreciative of such a kind offer.

I asked her to drop me off at the corner as it was going to really take her out of her way to turn left, when she needed to turn right to get back to her hotel. Melbourne City seemed quite confusing to me with its hook turns. As I got out, I thanked her for her kindness and for all the events of the evening, and, without a thought, I heard myself blurt out, "I love you." Oh, how foolish I felt! She may not have interpreted that the way I had meant it! It may have made her feel uncomfortable! So I quickly closed the door and took off on foot thinking, "you *idiot*, why did you say that?"

Think before you speak!

I went to sleep feeling that I had ruined a perfect evening. I was so disappointed with myself for that. I prayed that Hayley would not feel uncomfortable with what I had said to her and that she'd understand how I had meant it … not as some starry-eyed silly fan, or intimidating individual, but as a kindred spirit who felt a bond of true friendship.

The next day the train was not due to depart until 4.30 pm, yet I had to vacate my room by 10 am. How was I going to fill in the day? I arranged to leave my luggage with reception and offered them the beautiful flowers. They were delighted to have them and even more so when I explained where they had come from.

I ventured out, looking for something to fill in the time. I spent ages paging through books in bookshops, finally finding one that interested me enough to buy. I then found a quiet coffee shop where I felt comfortable to sit and read my book at my leisure. Indeed, I felt as if I were on holiday in Europe somewhere . . . perhaps a Parisian café. I was savouring the hot chocolate with marshmallows as I mentally devoured the book I had bought. It was Marianne Williamson's 'A Return to Love'.

After a while, I walked back to collect my luggage and set off early for the station. It was better to be there with plenty of time, to sit and read my newly bought gem of a book, than to dawdle now and rush later. I arrived at the station with one and a half hours to spare. As I mulled over my feelings regarding the last comment I had made to Hayley the night before, I felt uneasy; I was sad to be going home feeling like this. Then a thought flashed into my head, out of left field, like from a voice outside of myself—again. (I later learned that this was my intuitive voice of my higher-consciousness). Its message was to phone Hayley at her hotel to thank her for having invited me to the end of show party. That way the adventure would not end on this uncomfortable note. *Thank you, Voice, for this inspiration!*

I dialled the number of the hotel and asked the receptionist if I could speak with Hayley Mills. I was asked for my name and told to hold. Within a moment, and being taken quite off guard, Hayley's voice welcomingly sounded "Helen!" I quickly asked if I was interrupting her to which she replied, "No, I am just having a cup of tea on the terrace. It's lovely to hear from you—you couldn't have timed it better." I explained that I was phoning to thank her for her kindness in having me as her guest the night before, and that I had enjoyed every moment of it. She reciprocated by saying how special it was that I had come all the way from Newcastle to Melbourne just to see her. Our conversation really took off and we chatted about all sorts of interesting subjects, one in particular being the book 'A Course In Miracles'. We were both studying it and had lots to discuss regarding it. Hayley asked me if I had read Marianne Williamson's book 'A Return to Love'. How amazing was that? I was able to share with her that I had bought it earlier in the day and had spent a few hours reading it already. Our similarity in interests was staggering! Our conversation spanned well over an hour. It was such a delight for me that Hayley was chatting with me as a close friend, talking about deep and meaningful things.

Can you imagine, then, how difficult it was for me to have to say to her that I couldn't keep talking, as I needed to go and board the train before it left without me! In parting she said, "Helen, if you ever get to London, I'd be very pleased to see you again." I rejoined, "Oh, Hayley, now you've done it! There's a challenge for me! I have only two and sixpence, but mark my words, I *will* achieve it, as to visit you in England would be a further dream come true." I wished her well for her return flight home and reunion with her family, and we said our goodbyes.

I found my way to the train and, having settled into my seat, put my head in my book, anxious to explore it further to discover things that Hayley had spoken of. I spent time staring out of the window, deep in thought and in awe and wonder of the magical adventure I had just experienced over one weekend . . . a weekend that would live in the forefront of my memories for the rest of my life.

My prayer of gratitude: *Thank you.*

12) Hayley and John Frost at the after show party,
VCA, Melbourne, 15th February, 1992.*

13) With Hayley at the after show party, 15th February, 1992.*

14) Walter Van Nieuwkuyk & Christine Mahoney giving Hayley a ride on the wardrobe trolley to the car park, VCA Melbourne, 15th February, 1992.

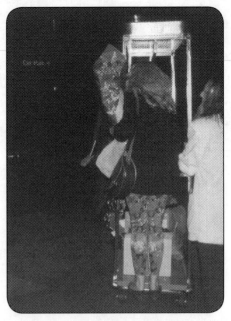

15) Hayley enjoying the ride.

PART FOUR

Another Time
Another Place

As time passed, Hayley and I exchanged some lovely letters of friendship. This friendship was no longer a fantasy; it was a reality. I knew I had achieved my dream—to be considered by Hayley as a true friend. She shared some very personal and private things with me, which showed me the strength of friendship that she felt toward me—she was so trusting and honest. Not foreseeing any further opportunity of adventures for me where Hayley was concerned, I settled into a state of happy contentment with this pen-friendship. I was in awe of her spiritual wisdom. I was humbled by her constant seeking of spiritual expansion. She was more Christ-like than anyone I had ever met before.

A friend invited me to join a small group of people who were meeting each week for six months to study Attitudinal Healing. At the end of the six months, it was expected that we would have the necessary knowledge to be Attitudinal Healing Facilitators. My personal development, from the time before I had met Hayley, until now, was quite obvious and I found myself on a quest for further growth. Hayley was such an aware being; she was so steeped in unconditional love, and was so much further down the path of spirituality than I was, that I now was thirsting to grow.

Although I was a practicing Christian, I recognized that my outlook was so narrow that it held me bound instead of being freeing. I had argued, with my Christian arrogance, against those who'd had a broader vision than me, stating that they couldn't be a Christian and believe in clairvoyance and karma and dharma and reincarnation. So it was that I joined this small band of personal-growth seekers. There were five men and five women along with a male and a female leader. It was a well-balanced group of intelligent, sensitive people.

One of the men was a former Catholic priest who had fallen in love with a delightful lady and, of course, the Church couldn't accept that. He had left the priesthood because of it. He was such a beautiful man—a man of integrity, emanating love and spirituality, and so relaxed with so-called religious dogma. Seeing him this way gave me permission to think outside of my conditioned religious square. I was inspired by him. I wasn't forfeiting anything, just daring to ponder ideas other than those upheld by the Church. This gave rise to my reading of books that I would have otherwise ridiculed, such as Dr Brian Weiss' book 'Many Lives Many Masters', and Jenny Cockell's book 'Yesterday's Children'—both non-fiction books relating to reincarnation.

While visiting Lori, my long-time friend from school days, we ventured to attend a Body, Mind & Spirit Festival in Brisbane, something that I would never have allowed myself to have done in the past. Lori was a lot more broad-minded than me. She hadn't had the Christian conditioning that I had had. In fact, her mother was clairvoyant. Yet we had been the best of friends since school days, always honouring each other with love. It was with my Christian bent that I was attracted to a stall at the Festival where a video was being played of a lady dressed in a style of liturgical gown, sermonizing. I stood watching for ages before I dared to ask for further information. I was met with friendliness and courtesy and certainly no sense of pressure to pursue anything. This gave me the freedom and sense of security to investigate more. There was a base in a Sydney home where one could access a library of books, tapes and videos of these teachings.

So again I gave myself permission to enter into a time of research. I spoke to a Christian friend about these teachings and was amazed to learn that she, herself, had already heard of them and, in fact, had visited this library on several occasions. This was the Summit Lighthouse, set up by Mark and Elizabeth Prophet of the "I AM" movement. Together we visited the library and made nice friends of the people who lived in the home that housed it. I found that a lot of what these teachings had to say made sense to me. It was no surprise then to find that the established Church to which I belonged criticized them as being heretical. The missing Gnostic gospels from the Bible had information that the Church didn't deem appropriate. I could see why! There was a lot of information that ultimately led to one being spiritually responsible and in control of one's own destiny rather than being controlled by the external inflicted dogma of the Church. I was going where the Church certainly wouldn't want me to go—*outside their boundaries and beyond their control.*

I came into a world that refused to be manipulated by unenlightened thought, and in it I discovered the God of Life and Light, not the tribal God of wrath. Finding the true Christ Consciousness so freeing, I decided to refer to myself as a Christ-light, rather than as a Christian. I was emerging from my caterpillar state into the butterfly. I became more aware of unconditional love and freer of judgements, mainly upon myself, as that's where I held most of my judgements. I felt so light. Of course I had my moments of regression into conditioned thoughts and behaviours, but I was now on a journey that I had no intention of halting.

The Attitudinal Healing Course was amazing, and, as if by coincidence, it came out of the teachings found within the book 'A Course in Miracles'. This is the same source book that Marianne Williamson refers to in her wonderful book, 'A Return to Love', which I had bought in Melbourne. Attitudinal Healing took us from the world's thought system based in fear into a spiritual psychology based in love. This love-base is what the Church promotes but what it so often doesn't deliver. Its premise is that "we are right and if you don't agree then you are wrong"—instant judgement! I found the Church very controlling and judgemental, whereas Jesus taught unconditional love, which is freeing.

Through my research, I came to understand that fundamentalists and fanatics exist in all religions, but they are not grounded in love. They are grounded in control, which is fear-based—the antithesis of love. God is generally seen as the tribal God, the punishing God, whereas the God that Jesus spoke of was unconditionally loving. The Kingdom of God is the Kingdom of Love. 'God is Love' was like a cliché to me, as it had been well ingrained in me for years, but only now could I say, "Got it!" *The Kingdom of God is wherever Love is.*

The disciples of Jesus in his day saw him as living within this Kingdom of Love, which was too radical for them to understand. Their religion was based on control. Jesus seemed to come from a different world. His world was a spiritual world expounding Love. Therefore it could only be that Jesus was of God. In this era of spiritual advancement, we understand where Jesus was coming from, but back in his days of walking this earth he was so far ahead of his time that to claim that he was the only Son of God, the Messiah, was the only explanation. Now I was seeing Hayley as being of this same Kingdom of Love, as she was an enlightened soul who was living her life from the premise of unconditional love based on a spiritual understanding. What a wonderful and unexpected journey I found myself on!

'The Amazing Valda' was a radio personality who had airtime on a Newcastle radio station on a Thursday afternoon. She was a renowned clairvoyant and, despite my religious background, I did enjoy listening to her. (I guess I was more open to her gift as a result of knowing Lori's mother). What she had to say intrigued me as she tapped into areas of people's lives in an uncanny way. I found myself wishing that I could have counsel from her. It seemed so serendipitous that only a few weeks later, while speaking to a friend, I learnt that she had actually had an appointment with Valda and was able to pass her phone number on to me. It was with nervousness and anxiety that I phoned and made my own appointment. It seemed extraordinary that, as a Christian, I should be doing this, but I felt the urge to do so.

Upon meeting Valda, I found her to be a very ethical and business-like woman. She was very matter-of-fact to start with, but as the reading progressed she seemed to enter into insights with genuine interest and concern. She told me that Hayley and I had been twin sisters in a past life, and that Juliet (Hayley's elder sister) and Gemma were also a part of that past life. She didn't elaborate as to what relationship they'd had with us, only that they were with us. She said that, although I wasn't a Hayley look-alike as such, there was a very strong family resemblance between Hayley and me and Juliet. (This shows up particularly well in a photo that appeared in the Sydney Sunday Telegraph of Hayley and Juliet, when compared with the small super-imposed photo of me, [photo 16]). Valda also said that, although I had been on stage, it was not my life path for this lifetime. She said that Hayley and I had both been Shakespearean actors in a past life, but in this lifetime I didn't need to be on stage as I was living drama! *Ouch!* Certainly my life hadn't been smooth sailing.

Here was this notion of past lives again. I had heard a highly respected Christian friend talk of her belief in past lives and reincarnation, fed by her own experiences, but it was all very foreign and questionable to me. How far was I prepared to let my mind stretch? I was being faced with ideas never before allowed into my consideration. So my personal and spiritual development was on a broadening path, to say the least.

It was in mid-February 1993, one year since seeing Hayley in Melbourne, when I received a phone call from a dear friend, Glen Barker, to tell me that he had inside information that Hayley was returning to Australia the following month. She and her sister Juliet were to star in a Noël Coward play and were again appearing on 'The Midday Show' with Ray Martin. Glen, an acclaimed magician, had many talents and had directed some of the stage musicals in which I had had leading roles. He was very involved in the entertainment industry. I was so excited to hear that Hayley was to come back to Australia that I set about thinking of how I was going to be able to see her amidst her busy schedule.

I started by phoning 'The Midday Show' and ascertaining the date of their appearance—12ᵗʰ March. I gave an account to the receptionist of how, last time Hayley had appeared on their show, they couldn't give me a seat in the audience, but this time I wasn't going to take no for an answer as I was a friend of hers and wanted to be there for her. Without hesitation, I was asked, "How many tickets would you like?" When I said "Only one", the receptionist was keen that I should have more, but no, one was all I could use. What a contrast to last time! Maybe I had got in early enough before tickets were given out to the bus company. I guess that would explain it. I then wrote two letters to Hayley. The first one I posted to her care of Channel Nine, and the second I took with me on the 12ᵗʰ March. My intention was to give the second letter to an employee at the studio to pass on to her so that she would know that I was in the audience even if my first letter had not found its way to her prior to their appearance on the show.

Gemma and I came down to Sydney from Lake Macquarie and I left Gemma with my mother while I headed out to the Channel Nine studios. Upon arrival at the studios, I found a large group of people gathering for 'The Midday Show', so I joined them. We were ushered into a room where we were to wait for someone else who would come and take us into the 'Midday' studio just prior to recording time. I seized my moment and asked one of the ushers if they could get my note to Hayley prior to her appearance on the show. He was very taken aback and wasn't sure about me at all. He looked at me very suspiciously, but I assured him Hayley would be pleased to get it. So it was that he left the room, my note in hand. The announcement was made for us to move on into the studio and take our seats. So we filed in and sat in the next available seat without any choice as to where that was. I realised at this point that I had been delusional to think that I could get to see Hayley here. The procedure was too rigid in its framework for that to happen.

We were approaching the ten-minute countdown when a lady from the floor hurriedly announced, "Is there a Helen Le Messs . . ."—"Yes," I quickly responded, jumping to my feet. Impatiently she signalled me saying, "Quickly, hurry, come with me."

As she led the way through the back corridors and across a vacant studio, she cautioned me to take care not to trip over the vast cabling sprawled on the floor. She warned, "We've only got a few minutes, you haven't much time to speak with Miss Mills, but she's asked for you." Just then I rounded a corner and arrived at a doorway where Hayley was standing. It was the doorway to the waiting room for all the guests who were to appear on today's show. Upon seeing me, Hayley gave me the warmest smile and opened her arms and embraced me. *Wow!* What an amazing moment for me! After a short while I loosened my hug, expecting that Hayley would too, but she didn't! She held on to me! *'What is this about?'* I wondered. *'Who cares, just accept this precious moment and go with the flow,'* I silently told myself. Eventually (I guess it was all of one full minute), we released the hug and started talking.

The lady who had brought me to Hayley interjected that we didn't have long. Hayley introduced me to Juliet who was sitting holding my letter that I had sent care of the studios, with the photo of Gemma that I had enclosed with it, on top. I bent forward and kissed her on her cheek and told her what an amazing honour it was to meet her. She smiled so warmly at me that I could hardly believe it. Juliet commented how beautiful Gemma appeared in the photo. I agreed, saying that she was the light of my life.

Hayley explained that straight after their appearance on the show they were being taken off for publicity photos and wouldn't be able to see me. However, she said that she would phone me when she could. She told me that the play they had brought here to perform was not planned for Sydney, only Perth, Brisbane, and New Zealand. I assured her I would get to see the show and that I'd come up to Brisbane for it. She actually seemed delighted that I wanted to do that and said she'd get me some tickets and that she'd phone me sometime. Just then the lady grabbed my arm and said, "We must go". So with a quick hug and kiss on the cheek with Hayley, and a wave to Juliet, I was pulled back to the studio, only just making it past Ray Martin when '3—2—1' was signalled by the hand of the floor manager. Ray started his introduction while I was still returning to my seat! What amazing timing on behalf of the lady!

Juliet and Hayley were sensational as Ray's guests. Upon their entrance, the applause was deafening. The girls were hilarious and the audience really enjoyed their sense of humour and candour. I saw Hayley unobtrusively scanning the audience looking for me, and finding me with brief eye-to-eye contact. After hearing all about the play 'Fallen Angels', I couldn't wait to see them in it.

It was with a heavy heart that I waved to Hayley from the audience as they were being applauded at the end of their interview. Hayley, seeing me, waved back. The audience, not realizing that Hayley was actually waving to one person, all waved back to her. So she and Juliet both waved to the audience as they exited studio right. I wanted to leave too, as I had no further interest in anyone else that day, but that wasn't allowed, so I sat through the rest of the show thinking of my future trip to Brisbane.

When I returned to my mother's, Gemma enthusiastically told me that she had seen Hayley on TV, presuming that I had missed seeing her. She didn't quite understand that I was seeing her in person while she had been seeing her on TV. I tried to explain that Hayley's wave at the end of her interview was actually at me, but the wonders of modern technology had been lost on Gemma. She was, after all, only five.

Two days later I missed Hayley's phone call, but she left a message on my answering machine. The message was that they were off to Perth and then New Zealand and upon their return in three months they would be doing the play in Brisbane. She hoped I was still intending to come up for it. I took the opportunity of sending flowers for their opening night in Perth, on 1st April, so they'd know I was thinking of them.

At this time I found myself deep in thought as to why I was so attached to Hayley. In fact there were three relationships in my life that I found hard to understand the importance of: The first one Hayley; the second one David, my former husband; and the third one Geoff, the love of my life, whom I had let slip through my fingers five years earlier. It seemed an enormous coincidence that, right at this time, I heard through a friend about a man, named Telynor, who was a church musician and who also read past lives! That was an interesting combination, even a contradiction in terms, I thought, yet obviously not to him. I sought him out for a past-life reading. I was not even sure that I believed in such a thing, but I was drawn to do this and went with my gut instinct—if nothing else, it could be interesting, and certainly fun.

The readings he gave made me feel I could have indeed experienced such lives. They didn't seem as foreign to me as I had expected. Of course, they hadn't come from my subconscious, so I just took them in my stride, thinking of them as interesting. The reading regarding a previous life with Hayley was indeed sad in its explanation of how my intense grief from that lifetime had made it imperative that I find her in this one.

Telynor had explained, "She was kidnapped from your side when you were both twenty-one and you never saw her again. In your grief you started a convent, dedicating your life to God. You couldn't cope with enjoying life without her, or with the guilt that, if you did live a life with the freedom to enjoy it, she couldn't. You never knew what happened to her and that is why your grief was so deep, and why it has been so important to you to find her in this lifetime." He also said that Gemma was with me in the convent, as my Novice Mistress.

Having been a nun in a past life would at least explain why, as a young teenager, I'd been intrigued by the nuns from a local convent, when I wasn't even a Catholic. I had been drawn to them like a magnet when passing them in the street, feeling the need to lightly brush up against their habits. It would also explain my interest in the Franciscan Third Order in my late twenties, and my initial thought of testing my vocation with the Poor Clares in my late thirties.

Although not the same, this reading did not contradict what Valda had said. Indeed the two could fit together quite easily. 'Yeah, well, who knows!' I found it all very intriguing, yet it still grated against my Christian background and there was a niggling of guilt because it wouldn't be approved of by mainstream Christianity. Telynor advised me that I was at the threshold of major spiritual growth, but that interacting with 'Christian Christians' would hold me back.

The thought of there being more to life than what I had grown up believing urged me to speak with a lady, whom I had met through conversation in a shop, who was, by chance(?), also a clairvoyant. She had given me her card so I phoned and made an appointment. On the 10th June I went for a reading. She was a local, middle-aged lady, very down to earth in her manner, and very friendly. Among other things, she picked up on a strong connection in this life with someone from a past life whom I had recently met, and how important this relationship was to me, and that I would be getting a long-distance phone call from this person very soon.

Upon arriving home I was gob-smacked to find a missed phone call from Hayley on my answering machine—this one from New Zealand! I was so disappointed to have missed it, but ecstatic at the same time that the clairvoyant had seen it coming. Here again was this past-life connection being spoken of. It seemed that I was being led to open my mind to its possibility in a more serious way. Little by little, the idea of a past-life connection was becoming more of a real possibility to me. The thought of it was mind-blowing; it was so way out there that it was fantastical. But what an amazing concept! Could this be what my attachment to Hayley was grounded in? There was no doubt that I was on a journey of discovery.

Even Gemma was coming forth with amazing insights. When she was six I was talking to her about my father (who died very suddenly of a heart attack in 1981—six years before she was born), and I was saying how sad it was that she didn't get the opportunity to know him. She adamantly said that she *did* know him—she used to sit under the tree with him and it was him who helped her decide to be born to me this time! Now where does that come from? Also, she announced to me one day, (after I had had the past-life reading by Telynor), that Hayley was her mother! I assured her that I was her mother—I knew because I was there when she was born! She shook her head at me as if I didn't get it. "No," she insisted, "not this time: Before. That's why I was a nun with you; because Hayley was my mum and when she was taken you had to look after me." This actually fitted with another comment Gemma had made when she was four. Gemma and I had both been ill and I had prepared a fruit platter for us to share. We were eating it while sitting at her desk, in the warmth of the sun, which was streaming into the room. She asked me, "Do you remember when we used to do this?"

"No," I answered, "we've never done this before."

"Yes we have—when we were nuns. Remember?"

*   *   *

I was actually home the next day when Hayley phoned again. The time of her coming to Brisbane was approaching. She told me there were now new plans to bring the show to Sydney (and Adelaide) and she thought that that fact would change my decision about wanting to come all the way to Brisbane to see her. As I had already planned the journey, and was looking forward to it immensely, I assured her that I would still come, but that she could well expect to see me at the show again in Sydney as well. She said that she'd also get me house seats for Sydney when the time came. This meant for me that there was now an added opportunity for seeing her yet again.

I felt excitement rise within as I sensed the potential of the unknown possibilities waiting to manifest with this new paradigm. As my mind was running wild, Hayley broke my train of thought by asking how many tickets I wanted for the Brisbane show. I told her that I only needed one as David was again going to look after Gemma for me. So she told me she'd leave the ticket at the desk of the theatre for me to collect upon my arrival. She also said she was looking forward to meeting up with me again and asked if I would like to come back to *their hotel* after the show and have supper with them. That's a *huge* step beyond meeting backstage or even the party invitation! Obviously I accepted her most welcomed invitation with great pleasure! *Thank you!* My gratitude to the Universe was immense.

On the 21st June, the day before the show, I took the overnight train to Brisbane's Roma Street Station. On this overnight train I was seated with a nice lady, a little older than myself. Although there was no reason not to get some sleep this time, I found that I was too excited to do much of it. What sleep I did get was light and interrupted by the lights of the stations where we stopped, and by people walking up and down the aisle as they passed on their way to and from the buffet car.

Arriving at the train terminal at 6.30 am, I lingered there, having a leisurely breakfast while immersed in a good book, before being able to check into my accommodation at 10 am. Once freshened up I telephoned a friend, whom I hadn't seen for twelve years, and arranged to meet him for coffee. I shared with him my life history since seeing him last and also the past-life reading regarding Hayley. He was somewhat bemused, yet, at the same time, concerned for me given my new-found broadening spiritual path and my embracing of thoughts on past lives and clairvoyance. He was Roman Catholic. He advised me not to share the past-life reading with Hayley for fear of her thinking I was completely gaga. I assured him that I had absolutely no intention of sharing it with her. To share it with her would be far too presumptuous of me.

It was lovely having time with my friend of yesteryear. We had shared much, thirty-something years earlier, and had maintained a continuing friendship of occasional contact since then. Yet I feared he found me too different from my earlier ways of sweet innocence and conservative religion for his comfort. Just as well I wasn't relying on his approval for the path I now found myself on. Isn't it interesting that when you grow beyond, or differently, from another, they feel ill at ease with your growth? It shakes their comfort zone so they have to assume you are getting it wrong.

However, I was glowing from the new-found awakening of who I really was and with that came a sense of confidence and purpose. Long gone now was my need for approval from others. Hayley's acceptance of me and her response to my friendship had lifted me into a higher consciousness—a heightened awareness of my spiritual being. It had breathed life into my ordinariness and given me a taste of a bigger picture of myself.

The hour of the show was approaching. This was not unlike the last time I had seen Hayley, in as much as I had travelled overnight by train and had not had any decent sleep. The good thing was that my hair was to my liking this time—right colour and right style [photo 17]. My eyes, however, were as red as last time, but I had come prepared with appropriate eye drops to dispel the Dracula look (I had learnt from my former experience). I made my way to the theatre by foot, having found a back-packers hostel very close by. I was feeling such excitement. My stride was light as if walking on air and the song in my heart was lyrical—in fact it was the 'Pollyanna Song'—and I heard it springing forth from my heart to my lips.

Upon arrival at the Lyric Theatre, I made my way to the ticket booth and to the girl serving there.

"I have a ticket to be picked up for Le Mesurier."

"Yes, Miss Mills left it for you." I sensed quite a personal touch here, complete with a warm smile. "You'll be happy with where you're sitting," she added in a friendly tone.

She was right. A better-positioned seat I could not have wished for. Hayley had done well to obtain this for me. How honoured I felt.

I didn't know quite what to expect of this play. Unlike 'The King and I', which I knew well, this play was completely unknown to me. It was Noël Coward's play 'Fallen Angels' and I knew from Hayley and Juliet's interview on 'The Midday Show' that this play leant itself to much fun and frivolity between the two actresses on stage together, so I was poised with anticipation for an enjoyable time.

Laugh? What a hoot! Even though I was there on my own, mentally and emotionally I was on the stage with them the whole way through. I felt as if I were at a party. I hadn't enjoyed myself so much since . . . I don't know when.

The highlight of my visit was fast approaching—meeting with Hayley backstage and supping with her at her hotel. It took me quite a while to actually find the entry to where she and Juliet were. Finally locating it, I was surprised to find it filled with people vying for Hayley's attention. Hayley greeted me but seemed preoccupied with the throng of others, so I suggested that I just sit over in a quiet corner and wait for her. I felt a little uncomfortable and conspicuous but, determined to overcome it, I sat down and opened my programme from the show and perused its contents.

As I did, Juliet came over to me. I think she sensed my state of not quite knowing what to do with myself and I really did appreciate her thoughtfulness. She greeted me like an old friend, with a warm hug and kiss on the cheek. I felt such acceptance from her with her warm and welcoming gestures. She had brought her sixteen-year old daughter, Melissa, who was travelling with the sisters as their dresser, over to meet me. I was so thrilled that Juliet did this as it gave me an even greater sense of acceptance into the Mills' circle. Melissa was so pretty and sweet, and an absolute joy. The three of us had a nice chat.

Eventually, Juliet said that she couldn't wait any longer for Hayley, who was still very deep in conversation with others, so she and Melissa would go back to their hotel and that Hayley and I could follow in another taxi later. Thinking that I wouldn't be seeing Juliet again, I gave her the gift of a little crystal that I had brought for each of the sisters. She was obviously touched by this and, without opening it, gave me another hug and kiss. Then, as they started to depart, she did so again. Juliet had evidently accepted me as Hayley's friend, and I was hopeful that she now also saw me as hers too.

At this moment, Hayley must have noticed that Juliet was leaving and, hurriedly excusing herself from the throng around her, beckoned me and we followed Juliet and Melissa out to the awaiting taxi. The three girls bundled themselves into the back seat, leaving the front seat for me. I felt so special leaving with Hayley and Juliet, and amused, that the on-looking fans could be curious as to who I was, and even envious of my obvious close association to the stars. Leaving with Hayley and Juliet made me feel important, but I knew in reality I was just a lucky duck. The taxi pulled away, fans and friends enthusiastically waving the Mills girls goodbye.

As we drove toward the Sheraton Hotel, Juliet opened her gift from me. Upon seeing it Hayley exclaimed that Juliet had a collection of crystals, so I was pleased that it was something she obviously liked. I was yet to give Hayley hers. That was planned for when we were having supper. Hayley asked how my trip up had been and she commented that each time she saw me I was on a quick trip and that I'd not slept for over forty hours! I said that it was because I came such long distances on overnight trains to see her, as she was so important to me. She softly and ever so sweetly replied, "Thank you, Helen."

I was asked where I was staying and, when I replied, "The Sly Fox", the taxi driver gave out a burst of laughter sounding as if he were choking. I guess the contrast of two beautiful famous actresses being taken to the classy Sheraton Hotel and their friend staying at the back-packers establishment was quite funny. I had to laugh too.

Upon arriving at the hotel, we stood in the foyer discussing where we would have supper. Melissa was tired and asked to be excused. Hayley ventured off to ascertain what was still open.

Juliet said that she'd go with Melissa and have an early night. It was already midnight at this stage.

I said to Juliet, "Please don't go on my account. I'd love for you to stay so I could get to know you better."

Her reply stumped me! "You and Hayley need time alone together."

What an interesting thing to say, I thought. It really struck me as quite extraordinary. *Why would she feel that Hayley and I needed time alone together?* I loved the fact that she thought we did, but it seemed so strange to hear her say so. It made me think that she knew something that I didn't.

Hayley returned and reported that the chef at the bistro was awaiting us. We said our goodnights to Juliet with hugs and kisses, and, with a knowing look from Juliet, and a returned curious gaze from me, she turned and walked up the stairs. Hayley and I went to the bistro and ordered our supper. Smoked salmon and avocado was my choice. On my supporting-parent pension such delicacies were a luxury and normally out of the question, but tonight was so special that I ordered it.

So, there we were, having 'time alone together'. While our order was being prepared, Hayley turned to me and, looking me in the eyes, said a most profound thing . . ."We've known each other for a very long time, you know." I was *stunned*. I sensed what she was alluding to. A wave of goose bumps attacked my skin sending quivers all through me. We had met only eighteen months ago. Even the earlier thirty years of friendship, which I had felt toward her, wasn't what I felt she was referring to here in her statement. No, I had a really deep sense that she was talking *much* longer.

I kept looking at her while all this was running through my mind, and I hoped that I wasn't showing my stunned disbelief at what I had just heard. Amazed, yet totally knowing it to be true, I eventually answered, "Yes, I *do* know." Hayley added, "We go back a long time. We've been together in a past life." I'm sure I would have choked on my food had I been eating. This was totally out of left field; this was the *last* thing I was ever expecting to hear from Hayley. We had been in another time, another place, together. It was so incredible that *she* sensed this. The fact that our connection was very real to *both* of us was the most validation I think I had ever had! Now Juliet's earlier comment fitted. Softly I said, "Yes, I believe we have. It's the only thing that makes any sense of all of this."

We had a very in-depth and thought-provoking discussion about conventional western religion and reincarnation. I explained how the latter was something that, as a Christian, I hadn't believed in, but my experiences with her, and my intuition, were telling me otherwise. My unswerving sense of attachment to her, since seeing her on the screen thirty-two years ago now, had to have a logical explanation. And there it was.

We talked about the values of our respective families, and how each of us was brought up and conditioned, and found our stories, experiences and values were so similar. I said that my mother wouldn't know what to do with this past-life theory of ours. However, on behalf of Mum, I invited Hayley, Juliet and Melissa to come and have dinner with us in September when they would be in Sydney with the play. Hayley playfully said, "I'd like to meet your Mum. We'll change her ideas on reincarnation—after all, we're proof of it!"

Can you imagine how I was bursting to share with Hayley the past-life reading I that I'd had, the transcript of which I actually had in my handbag? What to do? So, like diving into cold water from a great height, I took the plunge.

"Hayley, I've actually been to a past-life reader to see if he could shed any light on three of my major relationships which just can't be explained in normal terms. These are David, my former husband; Geoff, the love of my life; and you."

"Me?" she quickly exclaimed as her face lit up. "What was said about *us*?"

I explained that I had the transcript in my handbag, if she'd like to see it. She was most emphatic that she wanted to know what was said. So I read her Telynor's insights. She listened with great concentration, leaning forward at the table, and when I was finished she relaxed back into her chair, placed her hands, palms down, on the table and said, "Helen, I believe every word of that!"

"You do?" I asked, with surprise.

"Yes Helen, every word."

Words that Hayley had spoken to me on the first day we'd met came flooding back into my mind: "Maybe you had to lose *them* in order to find *me*": *Find her; NOW I had REALLY found her: We had found each other.* No wonder I had never been able to understand my attachment to her! We were more than kindred spirits, we were soul-sisters. That piece of the jigsaw puzzle of my life was now in place.

Hayley was also keen to hear the other readings, so I shared further. This led into more personal exchanges by both of us about our lives. I was now immersed in the friendship that I had always known existed between us. When I mentioned that my name, in my former 18th century life with David, had been Ann Millbank, Hayley got quite a shock. She placed her hand on mine and said, "Helen, there is more to this than we can understand. My mother has in her possession a ring from the 17th century with the inscription *Cornelia Millbank*. I think it's a family heirloom. It's a locket-ring with a small cutting of hair in it." Can you imagine how the goose bumps rose on our skin?

We talked on and on. Hayley asked me about 'A Course in Miracles'. She actually had a copy of the book with her in her room and said that she looked forward to seeing me again in Sydney, as she wanted to talk further with me about the 'Course' and about other books she was reading. We discussed the books of Florence Shovell-Shin. We talked about the Union strikes besieging Australia and London at the time. We touched on the possibility of Australia becoming a Republic, about the work Princess Diana was involved in with AIDS, and I expressed my sadness about the Royal family's debacles. We talked about religion and our own spirituality and spiritual practices. Karma was also a subject of discussion. We touched on the subject of Hayley's brother and my sisters, and of her boys and my Gemma. This was our true friendship in action.

I sensed the evening (morning actually) was moving on and that I should allow her to go up to bed. We had been talking for two hours. It seemed like fifteen minutes. It was at this stage that I brought out two gifts for her. The first was the same as I had given Juliet, and she appeared pleased, but when I gave her the second, an angel pendant, she was very touched. She read my accompanying note and commented on how much it meant to her. She said that the fact that I had a matching angel pendant made it all the more special [photo 18]. She asked to see them together as they actually face each other. So Hayley held hers up next to mine, which I was wearing. It was obvious she was pleased that we had them as something special between us. I was overwhelmed with her positive response to everything.

We then asked for a taxi to be phoned and, while we were waiting for it, Hayley mentioned that fans had an impression of her that she felt she invariably couldn't live up to—that when they get to know her she was not at all as they'd hoped. (*How could this be? She is an angel*).

I said, "When I met you, you were exactly as I *knew* you to be. You didn't let me down at all."

She said, "You flatter me."

"I don't mean to flatter you—I'm glad that I do—but I don't set out to do that."

"I know. That's part of what's so special about you."

She spoke about how special I was and how careful she has to be about fans, not knowing what she may find, but that she never felt that about me. She had a strong sense about me from our first meeting. She knew I was different—I wasn't like a fan at all—I was giving, loving and quite obviously a friend—a true friend. She added that she knew she could trust me from the moment we met, that I had a special-ness about me. She confided that she'd given me a lot of thought and knew that we'd known each other a *long* time.

I told her, "My life has opened up since meeting you; I have come to life!"

She was intrigued by that and asked, "In what way?"

I explained how I had found the true me again. I had given my power away when I had relinquished the pictures and articles of her, but that meeting her had brought out the true Helen and

I was back in life. (Now I understood why!) This touched her deeply. We hugged for ages, and then, looking at each other, we shared an intense knowing. Eventually I said, "I must let you get some sleep." She walked me to the door where the taxi was now waiting. A last quick kiss on the cheek and I was in the taxi, waving goodbye to my long-lost, but newly-found, soul-sister.

This evening has been the most extraordinary time of my life! I felt I was in a time warp as I travelled back to The Sly Fox. The details of my return train trip home have vanished into the ether, as I just wasn't present in the moment. I did get home, so I obviously did the appropriate things at the appropriate time, but it is all just a blur. In my head, I was still with Hayley at the Sheraton.

When friends and family asked how I had enjoyed my time in Brisbane with Hayley, it was easy to answer how wonderful it was. But, when they asked me about the details, I found I could only share the outline of events, as most of these friends were outside the spiritual growth that I had undergone in recent times. I could not tell them about my new-found connection with Hayley from a past life without the risk of ridicule, and I was not prepared to go there. I had a couple of friends who were actually ahead of me on the spiritual path from whom I found comfort through their total acceptance of, and their delight in, what was unfolding for me. But usually I kept what had taken place between Hayley and me very close to my heart, and rarely spoke of it to others. They simply weren't on that page. You may not be either. I honour you for wherever your spiritual path is taking you. I can only tell of my journey and what is real for me.

16) Photo of me super-imposed on a photo from the Sunday Telegraph (reproduced with permission) of Hayley and Juliet, showing the 'family' likeness between the three of us.

17) Having coffee in Brisbane, 22nd June, 1993,
feeling better about my hair this time.

18) My angel pendant—the match for the one I gave Hayley.

PART FIVE

Unexpected Meetings

It was now September and Hayley, Juliet and Melissa were in Melbourne with the play 'Fallen Angels'. After Melbourne, they were bringing the play to Sydney to perform at the Footbridge Theatre at Broadway. I was counting the days for their return to Sydney. I was delighted when, on the 19th September, Hayley phoned me from Melbourne to find out when I wanted seats for the show in Sydney. I had decided to make a special birthday treat for Gemma by taking Mum and her to see a Wednesday matinee of the play, which fell on her sixth birthday. I told Hayley of my plans and she offered to give us three house tickets for us to collect upon our arrival at the theatre. She also invited us to come backstage after the play so she could meet my mother, and see Gemma again, and so we could have a little time together and finalize plans for the dinner at Mum's. It was so lovely to see how excited my mother was over the thought that she, too, would be meeting Hayley.

It came out of left field! So totally unexpected! A phone call from Hayley on 26th September—*just for a chat!* I can't describe how this made me feel. Suffice to say that her statement of friendship made by the simple fact of this call was the icing on the cake for me. We chatted for over three quarters of an hour, mostly about 'A Course in Miracles', our spirituality, love, the Dalai Lama, the Findhorn Community, our relationships with our individual family members—a real friendship! We also touched on other things, including the excitement experienced by Sydney over the news of it being the chosen city for the next Olympic Games. Even after our time in Brisbane, I still found the friendship that she extended to me mind-blowing. I was consumed in wonderment at my journey since meeting her. I thought back, in awe, to thirty years earlier when I was busy putting pictures of her and her family up on my bedroom wall. How could I have understood back then why I felt such a strong sense of connection to her?!!

When the call finally ended, I entered back into the lounge room where my mother and Gemma were. My mother looked up at me with an inquisitive expression. "*That* was Hayley," I said with awe. My mother's eyes widened with surprise and she smiled with a softness that showed her understanding of what that call meant to me. Gemma made a few grumbling noises because she hadn't been given the opportunity to say hello to Hayley, but I hadn't given that a thought while I had been engrossed in the call.

Over the next week, as the day drew nearer to seeing Hayley and the play, and also to Gemma's birthday, our excitement was obvious. We talked about what we were going to wear; we consulted the bus and train timetable to ascertain what time we needed to leave; and Mum decided she was going to take a jar of her prize winning, locally sought-after, homemade marmalade as a gift for Hayley. It was so endearing seeing my mother getting as excited as Gemma and I were over seeing Hayley. My mother never thought that she'd ever get to meet her, even though Gemma and I had met her.

We arrived at the theatre and collected our awaiting tickets. Again, Hayley had arranged for us to have fabulous seats in the middle of the fifth row from the stage. I was really excited about seeing Hayley back stage again, as well as on stage, but also about seeing the play too, for it was so much fun and so entertaining. This play was very special to the Mills girls, as not only did they know the playwright, Noël Coward, personally, but he also was Juliet's godfather. What a fascinating life these girls had—Hayley's godmother was actress Lilli Palmer. Famous people were commonplace around the family dining room table. After all, their parents themselves were famous, and they had famous friends.

The play began and, to our delight, we found the intimacy of the Footbridge Theatre allowed us to feel we were in the actual room with the characters. I remember especially loving the song that Hayley sang in it—it was a theme that ran through the play—which I believe was 'Même les Anges', although after all these years I couldn't be sure. It was delightful to see how much a six year old could enjoy a play even though much of the content would have been over her head. The comedy itself may have eluded her but the comical gestures and expressions certainly did not. She understood the fun of the play. Apart from the times when my mother was laughing out loud, she had a grin on her face from start to finish. The grin was not only from the content of the play but also from her delight in being there, watching Hayley and Juliet.

When the curtain closed on the play, our hands were red and stinging from clapping so vigorously. Gemma had enjoyed it immensely and felt that seeing it was a great birthday present. We dawdled as we left the theatre, knowing we needed to give Hayley a little time before we intruded upon her backstage.

We must have been expected for, arriving at the stage door, we were shown straight through to Hayley and Juliet, who were in their small dressing room area. The welcome from them was wonderful. Gemma and Hayley hugged and kissed while Juliet looked on with the warmest smile on her face. Juliet then said hello to her and Gemma instinctively moved to her and put her arms around Juliet without any hesitation. Although Gemma had never met Juliet before, she felt secure within the atmosphere of the love between us all. She knew Juliet was Hayley's sister, and I had often spoken of her with affection.

Hugs were forthcoming for me too and held within them the sense of homecoming; so warm and welcoming were they in their strength. Upon introducing Mum to Hayley and Juliet she too received hugs from them. They responded with enthusiasm to being given the jar of marmalade, which I thought was very sweet of them. I guess not their everyday style of gift! However, it was one they genuinely seemed happy to receive. "A little home-style breakfast treat," Juliet had remarked.

Hayley then told us that their parents were coming to join them in Sydney during the week, unexpectedly, and it would mean that they would no longer be able to keep the dinner engagement planned at Mum's place. It was a very disappointing blow to Mum and me. The thought to invite them all to come for dinner fleetingly crossed my mind but that seemed too familiar, too pushy, like crossing over the accepted line. It also was too overwhelming for me and knew it would blow Mum right off the planet to suggest it. Our culinary skills were not elaborate and we were not at all familiar with vegetarian meals. I had undertaken the challenge to research such a meal to prepare for the girls, who I was aware preferred vegetarian food, but to add Sir John & Lady Mary to the equation was daunting to me. So I accepted their comment and left it at that.

After a little further conversation had taken place, Juliet handed Hayley a parcel, gift wrapped in birthday paper. Hayley then passed it to Gemma saying, "This gift is for you for your birthday from Juliet and me." I was so taken back by this gesture of kindness. Gemma beamed from ear to ear. She opened it and held up a pink striped pinafore dress and a pretty white top with a frilled peter-pan collar to wear under it. Gemma was thrilled (as was I) and thanked them with hugs. I too thanked them for their thoughtfulness and generosity. Gemma had no clothes like these. It was such a treat for her and she loved them. There was plenty of room for her to grow so they proved to be her favourite outfit for several seasons. Even now as an adult, so many years later, she still has them to treasure. Maybe a future daughter will love and wear them too. Being of the Oshkosh label, the quality garments have lasted the test of time.

Eventually, after a very chatty and lovely time with Hayley and Juliet, I thought we should leave before we outwore our welcome. So with hugs of farewell and words of affection we departed. We were so caught up in the moment that we left without anyone thinking to take any photos. When we returned home, we had birthday celebrations with a cake that my mother, who had been a sought-after wedding cake decorator for thirty years, had made and decorated [photo 19].

Two days later, Joy, a very dear friend of mine since primary-school days, arrived from South Australia to visit and stay with us at Mum's for a couple of days. Upon greeting Joy [photo 20], Gemma wanted to put on her new outfit to show her. Once she was dressed in it, Gemma asked if I would take her back to Hayley and Juliet so that she could have a photo with them in it. It seemed a wonderful idea to me! So I surprised Joy with the unexpected idea of coming with us into the city the next day and seeing Hayley and Juliet after the Saturday matinee. Joy, of course, was delighted. I phoned Hayley at her hotel mid-morning and asked if we could meet them for a photo after the play that day. She was very happy to do so, although expressed that they wouldn't have much time for anything more than having photos taken, as her parents would be at the show and they'd be caught up with them afterwards. Knowing that Hayley had all the family with her I quickly said, "I don't wish to intrude upon your time, Hayley; I will let you go back to your family."

"All right, Helen. I look forward to seeing you after the show then. Take care and lots of love to you and Gemma."

"And our love to you too, Hayley," I added.

"Bye," we chorused. Better to keep the call short and sweet. I could never get enough of her but the last thing I wanted was to intrude upon her time. I was still concerned that Hayley might grow sick of me.

Joy and I worked our plans for the day around meeting Hayley and Juliet at 5.15 pm. At 4.30 pm we arrived in the city to allow time to find a parking space. However, we found one easily, so we were at the theatre very early. We watched the patrons as they came out at the end of the play. It was obvious that they had enjoyed themselves. I had been so preoccupied with having Gemma and myself looking respectable for a photograph, having come into the city from time on the beach, that I had given no thought at all to the likelihood of actually meeting Sir John and Lady Mary Mills. But there they were!

They were standing on their own outside the theatre just talking together. Without much thought at all, I headed toward them. It was a bit of a knee-jerk reaction, like seeing someone you know and automatically walking over to them. I wasn't filled with thoughts of excitement, nor was I apprehensive as to what I would say. I wasn't thinking at all, I guess, I was just reacting. Reacting to the fact that Hayley's Mum and Dad were standing there alone and no one was befriending them. It seemed strange to me that here was a very famous man—with a face so well known to so many people—and yet no one was paying him any attention at all. So it was with immense boldness that I approached them.

"Hello, I'm Helen Le Mesurier. I'm a friend of Hayley's. This is my daughter Gemma, and my friend Joy."

"Hello, how very nice to meet you." They both held out their hands.

I continued, "For Gemma's sixth birthday Hayley and Juliet kindly gave her this lovely outfit that she is wearing and we have come to have a photo taken of Gemma in it with them."

"Oh that's lovely!" said Sir John. Lady Mary bent over to Gemma and handed her a beautiful rose that she'd been holding. "Would you like this?" Lady Mills gestured. Gemma, putting her hand out to receive it, said, "Thank you," and graciously accepted it. (Hayley later told me that she had thrown the rose to her mother from stage at the end of the performance. It was lovely that Lady Mary had then passed it on to Gemma). I then enquired as to how they liked being in Australia and they talked about having been here before and how much they loved it here. We chatted on and then Sir John said, "Let's have a photo together!" So he asked someone he knew who was nearby to take it. I handed my camera over and we all posed. Joy, feeling awkward in her beach shorts, ducked in behind Lady Mary while Sir John encouraged Gemma to stand in front of him as he placed his hands on her shoulders. I felt it was a very sweet thing of him to do. Although Gemma was holding the rose it is not visible in the photo [photo 21].

I talked of the great honour it was to meet them and how much Hayley had meant to me for over thirty years. I explained how becoming friends with Hayley had been like putting a piece of the jigsaw puzzle of my life in place as Hayley had a profound impact on me. I think the conversation would have taken quite a serious turn there as Sir John started to take quite an interest. However, just at that moment Hayley and Juliet emerged. Upon seeing Hayley, Gemma fled from my side and raced toward Hayley and into Hayley's open arms. I am grateful that I managed to click a photo without any warning! This fleeting moment could have been just that, but has been captured for all time on film and is one of our most treasured photos of a most treasured moment [photo 22].

I walked over to Hayley and Juliet, but Joy held back, standing with Sir John and Lady Mary. Both girls greeted me warmly with hugs. Hayley introduced me to their manager, Peter Adams, who had come out of the theatre with her and Juliet. This was so unexpected. I would not have felt it impolite of her not to have introduced us—as he belonged in her *private* life, and we could have been seen by Hayley as belonging in her *public* life—yet through this introduction she had drawn us into her private life. She had a way about her of making me feel that I mattered.

I mentioned to Hayley that I was coming to see the play again in two days time, only this time I was bringing a very dear male friend with me. Her voice was animated as she said, "Oh!

I'd like to meet a very dear male friend of yours! Come back after the show and let me meet him!" she instructed.

"Thank you, I will, but don't get too excited—*he* doesn't."

"Really?" enquired Hayley. "I can't imagine why not!" We laughed. She offered to give me two house seats for Gordon and me, but I had already purchased some, which were in the very front row, being the only ones left when I booked with such short notice. She was horrified that we'd be sitting so close up to the stage and suggested that I return the tickets and that she'd get two of the best house tickets for us.

Juliet encouraged us to get on with taking the photos, as they needed to think of their parents who had been standing by for quite a long time. They needed to be off their feet. I beckoned Joy over and handed her the camera and she took the photos for us. She did herself proud as a photographer [photos 23-26]. Hayley was so delightful with Gemma . . . it made my heart sing. Gemma quite clearly loved Hayley. I then introduced Joy to Hayley and Juliet and we had a quick chat. We then bid our fond farewells and walked away. Gemma was skipping, and although I wasn't skipping, my heart was. Earlier in the day I had not given a thought to the possibility of meeting Hayley's parents, nor her manager. What an amazing adventure this continued to be.

On the evening of 8th October, Gordon arrived at my mother's for dinner, after which he took me to the play. He too was looking forward to seeing the show and to meeting Hayley. Gordon was a very dear friend whom I had known, at this time, for seventeen years. I had met him through David and he had been David's best man at our wedding. Although the marriage had broken, he had remained a very dear friend to me. He was sweet and caring, always genuinely interested in people. When he talked with you, it was as if there was no one else around; you had his total attention and interest. He was like this with *everyone*.

After my divorce from David, Gordon and I had an unusual relationship. It was a very warm and affectionate one that could have been mistaken for more. In fact at times it was, even by me. It seemed to have the makings of going further, but never quite made it. I referred to it as a 'Clayton's relationship' i.e. a relationship you have when you don't have a relationship. He took a god-fatherly interest in Gemma, which was really nice. They got on extremely well. Gemma really wanted to come to the theatre with us this evening, so Mum had to work her magic in interesting her in 'a night at home with Gran'. Eventually, she succumbed to the enticement of games and ice-cream with hundreds-and-thousands sprinkled on top. So Gordon and I made our exit.

We collected the tickets from the box office and found we were sitting in almost the same seats as I'd had with Mum and Gemma. Gordon was very impressed with their position in relation to the stage. I derived almost as much delight out of seeing Gordon enjoying the play (at times almost catapulting himself out of his seat in hysterical laughter) as I did seeing Hayley and Juliet on stage again. I was so glad that I had invited him to see it. He had always taken an interest in my interest in Hayley and he felt very honoured at the thought of meeting her.

Upon setting eyes on Hayley back stage, Gordon's face lit up. He was totally swept off his feet by her. She was so lovely in her manner when meeting him, and he showed the same intensity of interest to her as he showed to everyone. Hayley made a few comments along the lines of how lucky he was to be my friend, egging him on in the hope of him taking our relationship a step further. He agreed with every flattering comment she made about me, while putting his arm around me in affectionate support. However nothing changed. To this day we still share the same warm and affectionate relationship. It has now been over thirty-five years.

Juliet was with us for much of the time but she was attending to other people as well, so she moved in and out of our happy little huddle tucked away in their dressing-room area. Then, out of the blue, Hayley presented me with a gift for my birthday, which was yet two weeks away. I was so surprised! She told me not to open it until my birthday so that I'd have it to look forward to on my special day. I thanked her with a big hug. How amazing was that! Now she had given both Gemma and me birthday gifts. I was so grateful for her love and friendship, yet still in total awe of it. As we were leaving, Hayley reminded me that I had the goal to come to England to see her and she said how much she looked forward to my achieving that. Now *that* was a dream *totally* beyond my capability to achieve financially, but I would not give up on it.

Our departure from the theatre held sadness for me as I wasn't going to be seeing Hayley, or Juliet, again while they were in Australia. I had, however, seen more of them than I had originally envisaged and for that I was deeply grateful.

19) Gemma cutting her birthday cake at home after celebrating her 6th birthday seeing 'Fallen Angels', 3rd Oct 1993.

20) Gemma greeting Joy at my mother's home, 5th Oct 1993.

21) Outside the Footbridge Theatre, Sydney: Me, Sir John Mills with Gemma, Joy (tucked in behind) and Lady Mary Mills, 6th Oct 1993.*

22) Gemma having run into Hayley's arms outside the
Footbridge Theatre, 6th Oct 1993.*

23) Gemma, Hayley, me and Juliet outside the Footbridge Theatre,
6th Oct 1993.*

24) Outside the Footbridge Theatre, 6th Oct 1993.*

25) A beautiful photo of Gemma (with the rose) and Hayley, outside the Footbridge Theatre 6th Oct 1993.*

26) Hayley, me and Juliet outside the Footbridge Theatre, 6th Oct 1993.*

PART SIX

Mountains to Move

A few days prior to my birthday, Gemma and I were watching the video of Hayley and Juliet being interviewed by Ray Martin. When in the interview it was mentioned that the play 'Fallen Angels' had been written by Juliet's godfather, Noël Coward, Gemma said, "I want Hayley to be my godmother." Leonie and Beth were Gemma's godmothers, but I saw no reason why she couldn't ask Hayley to be one too. I suggested that she could write and ask her, so Gemma rushed off and returned with paper and pencil and started writing a letter to Hayley. My heart was so touched by the sight of this six year old earnestly writing a letter to ask someone who was so special to her to be her godmother. I explained that she must not assume that Hayley would say yes, but that nothing ventured, nothing gained. I had been proof of that where Hayley was concerned.

With the letter finished, I was preparing to take it to the post office when I had another 'scathingly brilliant idea'. What if I could find a way to go to Adelaide and deliver this letter to Hayley personally? Maybe I could go and see the play again there and arrange to meet up with her and give her the letter? This would give me the opportunity of seeing Hayley yet again before she left Australian shores. Once she was gone, there was no hope of seeing her again. I had the dream of going to England to visit her, but I had no way of achieving that dream, and there were no future plans for her to return to Australia. This window of opportunity for seeing Hayley again made me feel like a puppy with a rag doll in its mouth shaking its head from side to side. I just couldn't leave it alone! But how could I achieve it? I didn't have the money to travel to and from Adelaide, nor did I know whom I could ask locally to look after Gemma for the week that I would need to be away. David was now remarried and living in Tasmania so I couldn't turn to him anymore. Of course I could always take her to Sydney to my Mum. *Think Helen, think!*

I phoned my friend Joy who lived at Port Augusta in South Australia. Although this was not Adelaide, I hoped Joy could help me 'shake that rag doll' some more and find some solutions. I needed to find cheap accommodation before I could venture further with any plans. I wondered if Joy knew of any such accommodation. As it turned out, Joy had a friend who lived in Adelaide whom she visited often and felt that I would be welcome to stay with her. Upon further thought, she came up with the idea that she could also come to Adelaide, meet my train, and we could both stay with Elly. Now, this was sounding good. My newfound dream was starting to take shape. So Joy made contact with Elly and phoned me back. We were both very welcome to stay with Elly for a week and the dates 11th–18th November suited her best. There was no way I could just produce the money required for such a trip, yet I couldn't let go of the dream.

I knew I had to find a way to attract the money to me. In total faith that the money would manifest, I did some research about dates and cost of travel to Adelaide on the Indian Pacific train. The cost was prohibitive. I was stumped! Then I remembered that I could travel to the New South Wales/South Australian border for $10 using my Supporting-Parent Pension

Rail Concession. Now I was on a roll! I phoned the Railway again and acquired an amended costing of the ticket. I was heartened by the result.

I mentioned to my mother what I was thinking of doing and she very quickly offered to give me money for my birthday to help offset the expense. She also volunteered Leonie to do the same. All I needed now was some money for incidental expenses like meals etc. and the ticket for the show. Hayley may well offer me a complimentary one but I couldn't assume that, so I had to make allowance for it.

Mum also offered to have Gemma stay for the week, or come up from Sydney to look after her, if necessary. I checked with Gemma's school calendar to see what she would be missing if she were to go to Mum's in Sydney for the week. Unfortunately, it coincided with an excursion, which I was reluctant to pull Gemma out of. She wasn't happy about missing it either, but more importantly she had a friend's birthday party she was insistent she wasn't missing out on. I suggested to Gemma that perhaps she could stay with a close school friend from Thursday to Saturday and then Mum could come and look after her until I returned the following Thursday. She liked that idea! I checked with the friend's family and they were very happy to have Gemma stay, even for the whole week. However, Gemma liked the idea of Grandma coming up and having her own time with her. Grandma would give her lots of attention! It wasn't often that Gemma had Grandma all to herself.

My birthday had arrived and with it Hayley's permission to open her gift. First, I opened the card. It had a picture of an angel on the front and inside Hayley had written: 'Dearest Helen—Happy 44th Birthday. What a perfectly wonderful age to be. This comes with much love and many, many thanks for being an angel to me. Hayley x'

Hayley was three and a half years older than me so I guessed to her forty-four did seem a good age to be.

Next the gift: I felt a rush of excitement as I carefully pulled away the wrapping-paper, exposing a hard-covered small-format book of daily spiritual readings entitled 'Opening Doors Within', written by Eileen Caddy of the Findhorn Community. I was thrilled with such a meaningful gift. Hayley had written an inscription inside it for me. We had talked about the Findhorn Community during her phone call to me at Mum's. This indeed was a very special gift that meant so much to me. However, I had a problem. Now that I had opened it and seen it, how do I contact her to thank her for it? I knew that they were taking the play to Adelaide, and I assumed they would have already left Sydney. I mulled over in my mind what action I could take to find out where she was and how to contact her.

Two days later, having had Hayley constantly on my mind, it seemed that my concentration of thoughts on her brought about another insight. *What if they hadn't actually left for Adelaide yet and they were still at their Sydney hotel?* I could attempt to phone Hayley there and thank her. It was well worth a try! So, it was with encouragement from the source of that insight that I phoned the hotel and asked to speak with her. With anticipation, I waited to hear whether the telephonist would ask who was calling or would say that she was no longer staying there.

"May I tell her who's calling please?"

Yes, she was still there! Brilliant!

"Please tell her Helen Le Mesurier is calling."

A short time later the telephonist reported, "I'm sorry there is no answer. Would you care to leave a message?"

"If you could just say I called and I'll try again later."

"Very well, thank you."

I phoned again two days later. Within seconds of my stating who was calling Hayley's welcoming voice was on the other end of the phone.

"Helen! How are you? Did you have a lovely birthday?"

I answered, "Yes, thank you, Hayley—made all the more lovely by your thoughtfulness in giving me that special book. I love it—thank you so much."

"Oh I'm glad you like it; I thought you might."

I asked when they were leaving Sydney for Adelaide and Hayley said, "We have the final night in Sydney on 6th November and opening in Adelaide two days later on the 8th."

Enthusiastically, I blurted out that my family had given me money for my birthday so that I could travel to Adelaide to see her again. At this point I had a heaviness of heart as I was fearful that she might be feeling I was becoming a bit of a nuisance.

Thankfully, she sounded genuinely surprised and pleased, and quickly added, "I'll get you tickets for the show. How many would you like and for when?"

"I'll be leaving Sydney on the train on 11th and it will take me two days travel to get there . . ."

"*Two days!*" she interjected.

"You're worth it, Hayley! . . . I think Saturday evening 13th November would suit well, if it suits you. I will be staying with two friends in Adelaide until the 17th. They'll come with me, but they will buy their own tickets." (It wasn't that I was trying to do my friends out of complimentary house seats, but rather that I didn't want to abuse Hayley's kindness and generosity).

"There will be *three* tickets awaiting you at the box office!" she insisted. "I tell you what, Helen, come backstage after the show so we can arrange a time to get together for a cup of tea before you go back."

"Thank you, I'd love to do that, and thank you for being happy to set aside time to see me again."

"Oh Helen, I'm so touched that you're coming on such a long trip to see me again," she exclaimed.

"Once you leave Australia, I don't know when I'll ever get to see you again, so I have to take advantage of whatever opportunity I can."

"Oh bless your heart," she said in a soft voice.

We said our farewells and hung up.

Ten days later, on the 6th November, I phoned Hayley again to tell her I was thinking of her, on this, the final night of the play in Sydney. I kept the call short, which she seemed to appreciate. She said that she looked forward to seeing me in Adelaide in a week's time, so that gave me a sense that she welcomed my calling. She always seemed happy to hear from me, even though I felt that I was imposing upon her time. This was my fearful thought patterning, which was not in sync with her loving thought patterning. I still had a lot to learn. It was interesting to me how, although I phoned her in love, I did so in fear of her feeling that I was a nuisance, yet my fear didn't stop me phoning her.

Feel the fear and do it anyway.

I wanted Hayley to know that I, her friend, was thinking of her—I needed her to know that she was so important to me. It uncovered an area within me that I needed to address and that was my sense of inferiority. The lack of being validated by important people in my life had left me feeling inadequate. Although I had a lovely friendship with Hayley, I continued to fear that she would feel I was pushing to build the friendship faster than was comfortable for her. Yet I had to embrace what time was available to me for it was such a small window of opportunity compared to the last thirty years. We were soul-sisters, and she was embracing me as such, yet in this lifetime she was a famous, revered actress and I was so conscious of that.

* * *

On Thursday, 11th November, I kissed Gemma goodbye at the school gate. I wouldn't see her again for a whole week. *This is madness,* I thought to myself. *I would never choose not to see her for a whole week!* Only Hayley was a big enough draw-card to entice me away from her for that long; before this we had only ever been apart for a few days at a time. Even when she went to Hobart to visit David, I had been part of the equation too, and had flown with her (at his expense) and stayed with them for the week. (At this time David and his new wife were expecting a baby—their daughter, Melissa—to whom I am now godmother. Amicable divorces are the way to go!).

I took Gemma's overnight bag to the friend's home and had a cuppa with the mum who was fast becoming a very good friend of mine (and who still is today). She then took me to the station where, with Gemma's pencil-written letter placed firmly in my handbag, I boarded the train to Sydney. After the two-hour trip I arrived at Central Railway Station to link up with the Indian Pacific train bound for Adelaide via Broken Hill.

Travelling cheaply left a lot to be desired. This was not a nice luxurious carriage, as I had expected, but an old 'rattle-trap'. I couldn't comprehend that such a carriage was a part of the great Indian Pacific train! I certainly had not expected such low quality for an overnight train trip. The Country Link trains were much nicer and more comfortable. Of course, there were very luxurious carriages as part of the Indian Pacific, just not this one.

My fellow travellers in this carriage were pretty rough. These people were not the type of company I was used to keeping; they all smoked and swore and were loud, but they were not threatening. As I had two days in their company, I decided I should accept them as companions. My efforts to be friendly covered up my despair at being trapped with them for the long trip, and their acceptance of my friendliness was very heartening. As is often the case, the rough exterior covered up a sincere heart. We chatted and laughed. They actually ended up being quite good fun to be with!

Judge not, and you shall not be judged.
(Luke 6:37)

Upon my arrival at the Adelaide train terminal, just outside of the city, Joy and Elly were waiting to greet me. I was so pleased to be with my friends, my style of people, again. I wasn't being a snob; I was just more at ease with them. On our way back to Elly's, we winged in through the city to collect our tickets for that night's performance. The three of us went in together and, as I asked for the tickets at the box office, a male voice from behind said, "Helen?" I swung around to see Peter Adams, Hayley's manager, whom I had met at the stage door in Sydney the day Joy came with us to take photos.

"Hello, Peter," I said, thankful that I had recognised him and remembered his name. I then introduced the girls to him. (Although Joy had been present the day that I had met him, they had not been introduced as she had been standing with Hayley's parents at the time). He asked if the three of us would like to join him at interval in a reception room for champagne. Wow—a chance meeting with him and we ended up being treated as VIPs!

He confided to me that Hayley was feeling somewhat deflated by a review in that day's paper, written by some mean-spirited journalist who had said some unflattering comments about her singing in 'The King and I' from two years ago. It was so unnecessary considering this was now an entirely different style of play. The thing this journalist hadn't taken into account was that Hayley was an actress who also sang, not a singer who also acted. Deborah Kerr, from the film version of 'The King and I', hadn't even been the voice behind the singing portrayed as hers. Yet here was Hayley, with a sweet voice, who did a sterling job of singing when it wasn't her main forte. She was a first-class actress who could also sing, but not as powerfully as this journalist had wanted. I felt so distraught for her. What meanness! I thought her style of singing was superb. I asked Peter to tell her so and to give her my love, which he said he'd do.

This journalist's assessment of Hayley's singing, however, was not the generally accepted one, nor that of significant personalities in the industry:

> Mills earns the approval of no less than Mary Rodgers, daughter of King's composer, Richard Rodgers. 'She really has a lovely voice. It's not a huge voice, but that is what amplification is for these days'.
>
> *Excerpt from article by Susan Wloszczyna,*
> *'Pollyanna Mills is whistling a happy tune again',*
> *USA Today, 12th May, 1997.*

So at 7 pm we three girls, all spruced up, arrived at the Festival Hall for a night to remember. Peter was in the foyer and, upon sighting us, came to greet us and escort us into a reception room for pre-show drinks. That was unexpected! When the chime sounded, indicating that it was time to take our seats, we sculled down the remainder of our champagne and headed off into the crowd as it was shuffling into the theatre. With great anticipation, the three of us, as arranged while enjoying our drinks, broke into applause when the lights dimmed and the curtain opened. We took the audience with us. Usually, I would have applauded each time that Hayley entered and exited the stage, but I couldn't do that with this play as Hayley and Juliet were rarely off the stage. The girls and I laughed and laughed throughout the play. We seemed to be more uninhibited with our laughter than I had been at the other performances. I think it was the fact that we were on a girls' night out and were feeling free to let our hair down to enjoy ourselves (the pre-show drink may have helped just a little!).

At interval, as invited, we headed back to the same reception room, where Peter was in attendance. He took us under his wing as he procured drinks for us and stood chatting with us for some time. I asked how Hayley was feeling. Peter said that, as a true thespian, she had risen above the newspaper comments and was quite obviously totally in character for the play. We all agreed that she was definitely in character—she and Juliet were entertaining us all a treat!

When the chime rang out again we enthusiastically returned to our seats. Throughout the play we had laughed so hard that our faces had at times been distorted, and by the end of the play our hands were stinging and red from fervent clapping. Joy and Elly were so glad that I had come to Adelaide to see Hayley and the play!

We wandered out into the paved area at the side of the theatre where I asked the girls if they'd mind if I went backstage to see Hayley on my own, as I wasn't at ease intruding upon her backstage with my friends. They agreed with my sentiments and waited for me while I went in to see her.

Hayley was surrounded by people but made me feel very welcome. Because of the pull on her time, she suggested that she take the phone number of where I was staying so she could call me the next day to arrange our meeting. I happily gave her Elly's phone number as we were walking from the theatre together, with Juliet not far behind chatting with others. We walked straight into my awaiting friends, so I re-introduced Joy to Hayley, and then introduced Elly to her. She was very warm in her greeting and spent just a short time chatting with them before she needed to leave. "I'll talk with you tomorrow Helen—sorry to have to rush off. Bye," she called as she rushed to catch up to Juliet.

Back at Elly's, we spent the rest of the evening, through into the wee hours of the morning, in stitches as we laughed over discussions of different aspects of the play and the interpretations of the characters by the actors. We sat on the floor lounging on big scatter cushions, feasting on pate, cheese, salsa and crackers, together with some fine wine, followed by chocolates and hot chocolate to round off the soiree. What a fabulous night of fun and frivolity! I was so glad that I had come to Adelaide!

I wasn't sure what day Hayley would phone me at Elly's so it was a lovely surprise when she phoned the very next morning. Her schedule was quite full and she was endeavouring to work out how she could fit me in to it. She offered for me to come to her apartment for a cup of tea the next afternoon but she would have to phone again tomorrow to confirm a time. I said that if it was too difficult for her to fit me in I totally understood, that I didn't want to be a burden. She assured me that I wasn't and that she really was looking forward to having time with me again. So the next day Hayley phoned and suggested I come for tea at 5 pm. It was the only time she had. I wouldn't have cared what time of the day she had offered me—I would be there!

I sat outdoors under a shading umbrella and wrote a note to give to Hayley. There were things I wanted to say to her and, since I was unsure as to which direction the conversation with her would take, I didn't want to risk leaving with these things left unsaid. At least I could just hand her the letter and she would have what I wanted to say in writing, which might even have a greater impact.

Joy drove me to the Ramada Grand Hotel. We arranged that she would wait for me by spending time at the beach directly across the road. I was sure I'd only be with Hayley for about half an hour. However, it was 6.30 pm before I reappeared. Joy was patiently waiting at the stone entrance to the beach, which was flanked by a low sandstone wall on either side. She was happy for me that I had been able to spend so much time with Hayley. Friends like Joy are a great blessing to one's life.

I had been welcomed very warmly by Hayley at the door to her apartment. She invited me in and, after initial greetings, gestured for me to take a seat on the lounge. Standing behind the dividing bench between the lounge-area and kitchen she asked, "How do you take your tea?" and proceeded to make it for me.

Carrying a tray containing quartered sandwiches and our cups of tea, she came into the lounge area and placed it on the coffee table in front of me. Handing me my cup and saucer, she sat beside me on the lounge at an angle, which I then sub-consciously mirrored. We sat informally, one knee bent up on the lounge with the foot tucked in behind the knee of the other leg. My flared skirt draped over my legs and down the side of the lounge, touching the floor. I felt very feminine and elegant as we sat there partaking in the chit-chat of old friends while sipping our tea and enjoying the sandwiches. *This was the manifestation of a scene that I had imagined years earlier, now playing out in my life.*

Hayley said how flattered she was that I had wanted to come all this way to see her again and how lovely it was to have some quality time together once more. As Hayley refreshed our cups with more tea, I retrieved the two letters from my handbag for her. I handed Hayley the letter from me first. After reading it her eyes looked up from the letter expressing a special softness. "You're a dear heart." Then with a spurt of exuberance she said, "Don't forget you're coming to England to see me!"

"Oh I'll be there, Hayley . . . I don't know when or how, but it's too important to me not to do it."

I then handed her Gemma's letter. "This is from Gemma, with her love." Her facial expression showed that it was a welcomed surprise. She opened it with enthusiasm and asked if I minded if she took a moment to read it. As she read it her face glowed with a warm smile and, with a look of gentleness and in a soft voice, she asked, "Do you know what is *in* this?"

"Yes, Hayley, I do," I answered.

"Oh my goodness, this is so special. To be asked by the *child* to be their godmother is not common; this is so special to me. How do we go about it? Do we need to go through the official channels or will this be something just between Gemma and me?"

"I have told her not to assume that you would agree to it, but if you are happy about it, then it is probably easier, given time and distance restraints, if it is just between the two of you, but it is entirely up to you."

"Yes, I think you're right. I'm happy to do it either way but if you think a private thing is all right, then that's what we'll do. I am so touched by this. There is something very special about Gemma and I will never forget what she said when I met her—it floored me!"

"What was it?" I asked.

"She said to me, 'I've loved you all my life', and at that moment I knew there was a connection between us."

"Oh yes, I remember her saying that in the doorway of your dressing room."

"Yes, that's right," she added.

"How do I let her know that my answer is a *big yes*? Should I phone her? Or jot her a note?"

"A note is probably easier than trying to match your free time with hers, and it will give her something tangible to cherish."

"Good, then that's what I'll do! Can you call me tomorrow just before midday and if I've been able to write it by then we'll arrange a time for you to pick it up from me? How does that sound?"

Well it sounded excellent to me because it meant that I would see Hayley *yet again*. I had envisaged that this visit to her apartment for tea would be the last time I would be seeing her for a very long time.

"That sounds lovely, Hayley, thank you."

At this point I felt that I should offer to leave but as I did so she emphatically said that there was no need for me to go yet. So, happily, I stayed a little longer. As 6.30 pm approached, I said that I really needed to leave for her sake, as she had to prepare herself for the evening performance. This time my offer was accepted and appreciated. Just in case things didn't work out for Hayley to give me the note the next day, I said goodbye to her as if it were our last time together for years. Sensing my emotions, she said to me, "I'll see you tomorrow sometime, I promise."

With a glistening of tears in my eyes, I waved as I walked out the door and down the corridor to the lift. I had been with Hayley again as her friend . . . a friendship steeped in the recognition of our soul-sisterhood.

As arranged, the next day, just before midday, I phoned Hayley. She hadn't yet had time to write to Gemma but hoped to do so between the matinee and the evening performance. She asked if I could phone again at 11 pm. Of course I agreed to do so.

Elly, Joy and I were still enjoying a choice bottle of red wine at the dining room table following on from a late sitting of dinner when the grandfather clocked chimed eleven. The phone was in the hallway so I left the room to make my call to Hayley. As I did, Joy called out that she was free to drive me to meet Hayley tonight if I needed her to. I really didn't think Hayley was going to want to see me at this time of night as she would be tired after doing a performance and surely would want to go to bed. However, I was wrong. She *did* ask if I could come over now to her apartment to collect the note for Gemma. So I said I could, and Joy happily drove me. It was exciting to be seeing her this late in the evening . . . what an adventure for me.

It was a lovely warm evening with a soft breeze that made you believe summer was already here. Summer was still fourteen days away but tonight was as a midsummer's evening. Even at the beach it was balmy; the sea breeze was gentle and not cold at all. I made my way up to Hayley's apartment while Joy stood across the road, once again, at the stonewall entrance to the beach. There was lots of peaceful activity on the beach and in the street and Joy felt very safe waiting there for me.

Hayley welcomed me and offered me a drink. She then handed me the letter for Gemma and I noticed that it was sealed. This meant that I would have to wait four more days before Gemma could open it and I could find out what Hayley had written. This was torture for me, but I honoured the trust put in me by Hayley and delivered it unread, unopened. We were having a lovely talk and I was feeling very much at ease. Hayley suggested that we have some photos taken together and arranged for this to happen. I was so delighted that she suggested this, as I was hankering to have new photos of us together [photos 27-28].

As we were saying our farewells Hayley was so sweet, assuring me that we would meet again; now we had found each other we had a lifetime bond which would bring us back together in the future. We hugged for ages, then we walked to her door, she opened it, I walked out, turned, looked at her with a sad smile, together we said "Bye" and I walked away. My heart was heavy yet at the same time I was so grateful for this extra hour that I had enjoyed with Hayley unexpectedly.

Joy and I stayed soaking up the sea air at the sandstone wall. It was fun to stand there listening to the sound of the waves rolling in, crashing on the beach, and to watch all the people out enjoying the lovely evening. We stood there for quite some time as I spoke to Joy of how I was feeling about leaving Hayley and the fact that I was not going to see her again now for a long time. Tears welled in my eyes and Joy gave me a comforting hug. We walked back to the car in silence. There was nothing to be said and Joy understood this. In her wisdom, she just gave me the emotional space I needed.

The following morning I left on the 7.45 am train bound for Sydney. The carriage still left a lot to be desired, but, besides me, there was only one couple travelling together in it. I left them to themselves, as I really wanted to be alone with my thoughts and memories. Over the two-day journey, I thought back over my life. The impact that Hayley had had on it was immense. I looked back in wonderment at the first sighting of Hayley on stage in 'The King and I' back in October 1991 and how I had sat sobbing at the close of the curtain. The closing of the curtain on Hayley was the catalyst that set off a reaction to the other closures that had impacted me greatly, the wounds of which were at that time still raw . . . the closure of my fifteen-year marriage; and the closure on any hope of uniting with the love of my life, Geoff.

I thought of the day I had met Hayley and the way that had come about. I had started out as a little mouse that had taken on its fear of the unknown. I had the courage to step out of my safe little world and reach for my dream when opportunity knocked. Now I felt the power of accomplishment. I felt the power of having faced the fear and had my dream fulfilled. I revelled in where my boldness had taken me. Who would have believed (*other than for David!*) that my boldness in going to Melbourne would have resulted in my being invited, *as her friend*, to the end of show party? I reminisced over the subsequent meetings with Hayley and the amazing conversations we'd had, especially at supper in Brisbane. That evening had changed my life forever. This journey to Adelaide had been another amazing adventure in the 'life and times of Helen Louise'.

Closures had become a familiar experience to me now. I had supplanted as many as I could by creating new openings, but this time there were no new openings to create. I had to accept this one, with its sense of loss, just as it was. The journey that I had so far travelled with Hayley had changed me though, and I was able to take this closure more in my stride, with a sense of excitement for the unknown future.

But still, there it was . . . another closure.

27) With Hayley in Adelaide, 16th Nov 1993.*

28) With Hayley in Adelaide, on the balcony of her apartment with the night ocean backdrop, 16th Nov 1993.*

PART SEVEN

Searching for the Self

It was with much excitement and anticipation that I handed Hayley's letter to Gemma to open. With the letter was an autographed photo, which read:

For Gemma ~ With all my 'special' love from your honorary God-Mother ♥ Hayley ♥ xxxxoooo.

Gemma clutched the photo to her chest. This gesture melted my heart. I picked up the letter and opened it out and handed it to her, allowing her to try to read it for herself, but she soon handed it over to me to read to her. It was the most beautiful letter I had ever read. Hayley had signed it 'God bless you little darling. I love you too. Your own special honourary God Mother, Hayley xx'. So, although there had been another closure when leaving Adelaide, here was another new beginning... the beginning of the relationship between Hayley and Gemma. This was like handing down a family heirloom. Now, not only did I know Hayley as my soul-sister, but also as my daughter's godmother. Her loving response to Gemma had transcended the relationship that Hayley and I shared. It had now given birth to a new relationship.

I felt so validated by Hayley's friendship and loving acceptance of us in her life. My boldness had rewarded me many times over. It had given me such a sense of wholeness. I had become a self-assured, happy person.

*   *   *

New Year's Eve 1993 saw me with a list of resolutions for the New Year. Somehow I had to attract into my life the means by which to take Gemma and myself to England to visit Hayley. I had also told Gemma that I would take her to Disneyland before she left primary school, but I had no idea how I was going to do either! I couldn't make a promise to Gemma and not keep it, so this was my way of making sure I focused on it, knowing that what you focus on is what you attract. This coming year needed to be a year that moved me forward in a very positive way, drawing on the energy derived from the experiences with Hayley. I knew that I wanted this to springboard me into an era of assertiveness and motivation that would enhance my life.

I launched 1994 by enrolling part-time in the Travel Certificate course at the local TAFE. The classes were held during school hours so fitted in well with being home with Gemma after school and in the evenings. I did very well in this course and was encouraged by my teachers to continue on for another two years and do the Advanced Certificate. I felt that it would be a good example for Gemma to see her mother applying herself to her studies, showing her how to apply herself to homework and study in the future. A friend made a sign for my desk that read 'Mature-age Student Extraordinaire.' It seemed to work on me as I topped the course with High Distinction. It really was interesting to observe how students straight out of school and entering tertiary study weren't focused in the manner I was. The maturity certainly gave me the edge. I was there to learn and achieve to the best of my ability, whereas most of the others were there because they had to be somewhere!

Unfortunately, having this qualification didn't actually help me. I only wanted to work part-time as I still wanted to be the mother who was at home when my daughter left for school and there for her when she came home. I hadn't realized that Travel wasn't an occupation where you could work part-time to start with. This was something only those who had a lot of first-hand experience and knowledge in the field were privileged to. So the expected outcome (employment) didn't eventuate. Still, it had given me a sense of achievement, and that in itself was of value. However, I was no closer to visiting Hayley.

Although 1991 had been the start of this new era of personal and spiritual growth in my life, it was way back in 1981, when my father was taken from our midst so abruptly, that I first began seeking answers to spiritual questions. I had an especially close bond with him and I went to pieces at the news of his death. I was living in Perth at the time, and he died in Sydney. Due to the distance, I had only seen him once in the past year, and just to get home to my family now I would have to undertake the four and a half hour flight to Sydney. To add insult to injury, this had seemed a good time for the domestic airlines to hold a strike (after all, it was Holy Week, leading into Easter—what better time was there to hold a strike?).

Qantas International managed to kindly accommodate me. Although they were not allowed to take domestic passengers, they booked me through to New Zealand on their flight from London to New Zealand, which was touching down in both Perth and Sydney. Upon my return to Perth I would be able to receive a refund for the part of the flight that I wasn't undertaking (Sydney-New Zealand). Unfortunately David was unable to accompany me because he had an enormous responsibility to

143

the Cathedral for their Liturgical Easter music—something my father would have totally understood.

I touched down in Sydney to discover that Dad's funeral was being held just four hours later! Deep in my grief and concern for my mother I had given no thought at all to a funeral. The synchronicity of the timing intrigued me. Further, had it not been scheduled for that day, the funeral would have had to have been on the following Tuesday (due to the Easter weekend holidays), by which time I would have to be back in Perth as David and I were flying out to London on the Wednesday for him to sit the Choir Master's examination at the Royal College of Organists in London.

My thirst to know where Dad now was (for I knew death was not the end of life), along with this sense of divine timing, led me to a book 'Life After Life' by Dr. Raymond Moody. It offered insight into near-death experiences. Thankfully, it gave me some peace and opened my mind to other spiritual ideas. However, it was 1995 that saw a new burst of accelerated growth, which urged me forward on the path of self-development, personal empowerment and spiritual evolvement.

Even though I'd had periods of empowerment before, enabling me to separate from David in 1987 and again in 1989, I hadn't had the personal growth I needed to maintain my empowerment and to bring my life into balance, so matters with him had been left unresolved. My new path had begun on the day I first saw Hayley on 'The Midday Show' in May 1991; it had sparked something in me. Four months later, David and I had parted permanently and amicably. We were more like brother and sister now for the love didn't change, only the form it took. I had come into a period of *my time*. It was now *my time* to really enjoy being a mother to Gemma and freeing myself of other stresses. It was time for me to discover who I really was ... me, the free, unfettered, me!

This had led me to self-examination and evaluation. I had found a kind girl who was eager to please, eager to conform to fit in with society and the Church, and eager to do what was expected of her. I became aware that my inner talk held lots of 'shoulds'! I recognised that while being moulded as a youngster from a spirited child into a placid child, the real me had in fact been suppressed. My sense of Self had been stumped. I had tried to live my life to please others. That was up until 1991 when David's attitude to me over Hayley had flipped me over into a state of self-determination. It was then that the real Helen had started to push her way out of the cocoon. Up until then, I had always taken the 'right' fork in the road, making choices that were expected of me and reacting to the 'shoulds' that pleased others. Now I had found the key, which I had turned, resulting in freedom of spirit to choose the 'left' fork in the road—the path of my heart's desires.

In the past I had made choices that pleased others by using the rationality of my head and denying my heart. I had tried so hard to appear mature, all the time feeling insecure and unsure of myself ... a scared little girl being set adrift on the raft of life with no rudder or paddle.

Musical theatre was the way I engendered some self-esteem. I was very confident when playing the role of someone else, but I had no one to hide behind when I was just being 'Helen' singing at eisteddfods, weddings, etc. However, it was the only area in which I felt I had anything to offer and where I felt I was validated. I took lessons in piano and singing, and, although

I enjoyed playing the piano, I loved it when my father would accompany me while I sang.

In 1965, at age fifteen, I was handed the leading role in Gilbert & Sullivan's 'The Pirates of Penzance'. In 1966 I was away with my parents overseas. On our north and south bound voyages aboard the 'Fairstar' I had enjoyed participating in their entertainment evenings and occasionally was asked to sing for the passengers. Over the following three years I had leading roles in the Gilbert & Sullivan shows 'Ruddigore', 'Patience' and 'The Gondoliers'. I then moved and joined the Gosford Musical Society, having the leading roles in 'Carousel', 'New Moon', 'Anything Goes' and HMS Pinafore [photos 29-40].

In 1974, I moved again, this time to Armidale, to live closer to a friend. It was there that I joined the Cathedral choir and met David, who was the choirmaster and organist, and I married him in 1977. Our lives revolved around making church music, which was wonderful and very comfortable to me as it had the vibration of my upbringing. I also enjoyed participating in a Music Hall production for which David did the musical direction [photo 40]. Our marriage lasted fifteen years, on and off. I lived to please him and our families, always taking the 'right' fork in the road.

Once Geoff and I had become aware of our love, our journey also took the path of the 'right' fork, *trying* to do what was expected of us. At that time Bishops had the power over our lives. We tried to get our acts together but it was impossible when we allowed the 'shoulds' into our decision-making. We wasted so much time pining for each other. It wasn't until 2006, twenty years later, that we were married [photos 41-43].

In the intervening years both of us had split from our spouses, but synchronicity eluded us during those years. We both ended up remarried to another, having relinquished any hope of ending up together. Further heartache was ahead in both these new marriages. The 'left' fork would have alleviated so much of that pain in our lives, but due to the clerical collar that Geoff wore he stayed in an unhappy marriage for far too long. Meanwhile my remarriage lasted only six months, as I had grown to love myself too much to put up with abusive nonsense from a partner. I chose the 'left' fork at that time, as I no longer was concerned with what others thought of me. In fact, I found that many were actually in awe of my personal empowerment.

How do I thank Hayley for being the catalyst that steered me on to the 'left' fork and into my emerging journey of self-development, personal empowerment and spiritual evolution? It was the importance of having her in my life that had pushed me into following my heart and taking the 'left' fork. This was the real me. This was me being honest about who I was at my core. It had empowered me with passion to act boldly, appearing totally out of character, yet actually being totally in character with my essence. I could have easily taken the 'right' fork again when David ridiculed me about phoning 'The Midday Show' to try to get into the audience to see Hayley that first time. I could have recoiled and done nothing further about it. I shudder to think what my life would now be like if I had stuck with the 'right' fork.

The following quote of Hayley's mirrored my insecurities but also my actions where she was concerned.

'I was quite a shy person,' she says, 'wary of being rebuffed and laughed at. Then there was this strange metamorphosis. Love emboldens. I acted in a way I had never done before.'

Excerpt from article by Fred Hauptfuhrer,
'Pollyanna never had it so happy'
People Weekly Magazine, 14th April, 1975.

My love of Hayley had certainly emboldened *me*! I too had acted in a way I never had before. My bold determination in my pursuit to meet Hayley caused me to act differently from how others would have expected, and indeed, even differently to how I would have expected.

Now I was on a quest for a bigger understanding of life. I was inspired by what Marianne Williamson had written about in her book 'A Return to Love', and how it fitted in with all I had learned in the Attitudinal Healing course. I had been introduced, through the Attitudinal Healing course, to the writings of psychiatrist Gerald Jampolsky. He had been given the manuscript of 'A Course in Miracles' to read prior to its publication and it had totally turned his life around. As a result, he opened a hospice in Tiburon, California for terminally ill children where he taught them the principles of 'Attitudinal Healing'. We had been shown a video of the hospice where some of the children had been interviewed. They were absolutely amazing in their understanding of love and life. There was not a dry eye among us in the class that evening.

I had developed the desire to be able to impact others' lives for the better and to give something of significance. I didn't know what . . . but my connection with Hayley had broadened my belief in myself—my belief in being able to attract whatever I felt really passionate about. My friendship with Hayley was the proof of that. 'A Course in Miracles' had triggered a shift in my consciousness—it had indeed brought about attitudinal healing. I had developed a sense of wellbeing with all the variety of emotions that flowed through me. I recognised that I wasn't my emotions; I was more than that: I was the awareness that witnessed my emotions. It was a new adventure to *watch* my emotions as they surged and retracted like waves on the beach. I was different now.

I felt an air of anticipation of something, but again, I didn't know what. I was continuing with my research into Elizabeth Clare Prophet's teachings, but, although they fascinated me, I knew that this was not what would take me in the new direction I was looking for. I was looking to find my life-purpose, which I instinctively knew would involve teaching Love. How to do that? I had no idea!

When the student is ready, the teacher appears.

Then it came, out of the blue. I saw an advertisement on television for a free evening lecture on the subject of the power of the mind, given by Michael Rowland. The subject of this free evening lecture intrigued me so I made sure I attended. This lecture was a glimpse into what Michael's upcoming weekend seminar offered. What Michael had to say fascinated me. I wanted so much to learn more about this subject, but I was up against the cost of attending the weekend course.

At the end of the evening, Michael invited people to come up to him if they had questions. I went up to him and said how much I needed to attend his weekend to learn this work but I didn't have the money up front to do so. In a very sympathetic and caring voice, he asked what I would like him to do to help me. I boldly asked if I could pay a portion now and pay the remainder of the cost of the course off over the next three months. He immediately accepted my request. I was amazed at myself for daring to ask such a thing and even more amazed that he so willingly agreed. (I later learned that Michael was Australia's leading personal development seminar presenter. He has since personally taught his work to Sarah Ferguson at her request, and he and his wife have enjoyed tea with Fergie and Princess Diana! He has written a best-selling book "Absolute Happiness" and has presented his seminars to over 220,000 people. In 2010, he wrote, directed and starred in his own film about the power of the mind, 'Being In Heaven', the premier of which Geoff and I attended in the thriving seaside resort of Byron Bay. His website is www.successlovefreedom.com).

So, in September 1995, with great enthusiasm, I attended his 'Life Essentials' weekend seminar in Newcastle. This seminar opened up a new world to me. All that Michael taught enthralled me. It was mind blowing—literally—it blew open my mind to its amazing power. I was in awe of Michael's knowledge and soaked up every word he spoke. He taught us of Hal and Sidra Stone's amazing work on the psychology of 'Sub-personalities and Voice Dialogue', which fascinated me. He also touched on meditation, which I had never given any thought to.

Four years later, I attended one of his Meditation Workshops at his property in the Blue Mountains [photo 44]. This was conducted in an acoustic 'shell' that he had acquired from the music department of a university. We learnt several methods of meditation but it was when we chanted to the increasing rhythms of the African drums that I experienced such bliss! A state I had never experienced before. I had never really meditated before, but I found that it brought such peace and tranquillity into my life, as well as many unexpected insights.

During Michael's 'Life Essentials' seminar of September 1995, one girl asked a question that resonated with me. She asked, "What if you choose to attract something into your life, by using the techniques being taught to us, that isn't what God wants for you . . . can you override God's will for your life by your own will?" Michael's response held such wisdom. He said: "God, Spirit, the Universe, call it what you will, speaks to you through your passion—your heart's desire. What else is it? To sacrifice your heart's desire for a more noble outcome is to do what others expect of you—the 'shoulds'. 'Shoulds' are never the correct action for you. They come from fear. The correct action is always from your heart. The action you choose may be the same, but unless it comes from Love, it is coming from fear." Michael made so much sense! How obvious was that explanation? If only my Christian conditioning had allowed me this understanding! But on the contrary, it had advocated sacrifice.

I came away and immediately put into practice the techniques that he had given us. I had learnt that while ever we had limiting beliefs then our lives were impacted by limitations. So my work was to release the limiting beliefs that I could recognize. These were obvious. I only had to look to the areas of my life that were lacking or limited and there, I knew, I held limiting beliefs. Michael had given me the knowledge and the tools to build on and to grow from. I was indebted to him for what he had taught.

Gradually my life became full of positive self-talk, upheld by loving energy. All that I had learnt through 'Attitudinal Healing' came to the fore and I was so energized with the life-force. I spoke and acted positively and lovingly without any forethought to do so. I gained a greater understanding of my connection to God and God's connection to all living things. I discovered that my loving essence was the image of God within me. ("God created man in his own image" (Genesis 1:27)). God and I were actually one. Now, I know that to many that idea seems arrogant and indeed blasphemous, yet it was so obviously true to me once I had gained this spiritual insight.

I was amazed at how far I had travelled from being the good Christian girl of the established Church. I realized how little of God was in fact found in the Church. I was so liberated when I understood that the 'Good News' that Jesus asked us to share with the world was not that he died on the cross for our sins and that we would go to hell if we did not accept him as our Lord and Saviour, but rather, the 'Good News' was that God was unconditionally loving! God was Love . . . not the punishing, fearful God of the Old Covenant of Moses, but the loving, merciful, accepting, and forgiving God of the New Covenant of Jesus. No one was *going* to Hell! Hell was a state of mind. It was the state where we absented our consciousness from God, from Love (or at least where we failed to recognise God/Love within us).

How freeing was that understanding? Love was freeing; therefore God was freeing, not controlling as often found in the institution of the Church. The Church taught one thing, and then acted in ways contrary to those teachings. There was such bigotry within the Church. The Church treated people with harsh judgement, whereas Jesus accepted people and told them not to judge others. The Church taught that one should live as Jesus did but didn't teach actually *how* to do that nor did they lead by example.

I recognized that 'Attitudinal Healing' was teaching us *how* to live as Jesus lived. This was through Love, not through fear, which was the way of the world. ("My Kingdom is not of this world" (John 18:36) refers to the Kingdom of Love). That now made so much sense! Can you imagine hanging from a cross and praying that the perpetrators be forgiven for they didn't understand what they were really doing? ("Father, forgive them, for they do not know what they do" (Luke 23:34)). What an incredible understanding of Love. So, when we came up against people who were intent on giving us a hard time, if we were tolerant of them (because they didn't really understand what they were doing—how they were living by fear not by love) and forgave them for their attitude (which in fact was against themselves as well as us), then we would experience "the Peace of God, which surpasses all understanding" (Philippians 4:7) and our experience would bring us inner joy along with that peace. Heaven really is within ("The Kingdom of God is within" (Luke 17:21)).

As this new spirituality was blossoming within me, I became aware also that New Age spirituality was indeed very necessary for our evolution. It empowered Love to permeate our consciousness. Love (God) was all there was and that was what the New Age was all about.

It was around this time that I stumbled on Shirley MacLaine's book 'Out on a Limb'. I had always loved Shirley. I admired her acting, singing and dancing and owned several of her authored books. I was spellbound by 'Out on a Limb' and couldn't put it down. It spoke of so much that I had been discovering for myself. Where others ridiculed her, I completely understood where she was coming from. I admired so much the way she allowed people the right to their beliefs but never allowed them to undermine her own. She didn't attack those attacking her; she courteously let them alone in their unbelief and misunderstanding of her spiritually. ("Father forgive them for they do not know what they do"). I thought her to be a woman before her time. She had grown into such insight and understanding of matters spiritual, including knowing that she knew so little of what there was to know, whereas others arrogantly thought that they knew it all and had all the answers. Wouldn't the world be in a better state today if everyone was tolerant of one another?

I knew I had grown into being a better person. Hayley's spiritual beauty had been such an inspiration to me. I could see a little more of the love that I had witnessed in Hayley now manifesting in me, and I knew that was a very good thing indeed. My heart's desire was to be the vessel through which others felt Love, as had been my experience through Hayley. The purpose for me having to find her in this lifetime was now so apparent. I was to learn so much from her. I was passionate that this Love would be what others would find significant in me. So I continued to work on my personal and spiritual development.

During this time, Hayley sent me a copy of Juliet's book, 'Body, Mind and Spirit in Balance', which Juliet had autographed for me. I was so touched by this and enjoyed the book immensely. It supported much of what I was learning from other sources and brought some fresh insight as well. It was as though the Universe was bringing before me all that it knew I needed. I learnt so much more about Juliet's beauty from reading this book. I would have enjoyed getting to know her better when she was in Australia, for she too was very spiritually minded, and had a wicked sense of humour!

My aspiration to get to England to visit Hayley spurred me on. I knew I needed to attract money to be able to afford to travel. So I chose to put into practice two of the techniques Michael had taught. The first one was known as 'vibrasonics' where, after putting yourself in a mental and emotional state of wellbeing, you visualised a thirty-second video clip of yourself experiencing your ultimate desired outcome. You repeated this video clip in your mind's eye ten times, thereby taking five minutes. You did this technique daily. My mental video clip was of being with Hayley in her home, enjoying our friendship.

The second technique, known as 'seventy times seven', involved writing a short statement of your desired outcome e.g.: 'Money now comes to me in abundance in perfect ways'. On the next line you wrote the very first thing that came into your mind—whatever it was: "Wouldn't that be nice" or "There is no way that's going to happen" or "Oh I forgot to phone Pamela". It didn't matter what it was. The important thing was just to write it down. The short statement of the desired outcome was repeated, followed by the next thing that came into your mind. You repeated this seventy times for seven days. There was also a shorter version where you repeated it twenty two times for eleven days. After leaving a break of however many days you'd done it for, you could do it all over again if your desire hadn't manifested. Your responses were the way your subconscious mind purged its limiting thoughts. Once you got past all the 'monkey chatter of the mind', the real limiting thoughts came to the fore and you just let them go. There was no need to examine them. They were out, that's all that mattered. Once there were no beliefs left in your sub-conscious mind against your desired outcome you would find it manifested very quickly.

As I proceeded with this process, it came out that it wasn't money that I wanted but the experiences that money could give. My responses showed just what experiences I desired. Of course I desired for us to visit Hayley in her home; I desired for Gemma to meet our relatives in England and for us to have time staying with them; and I desired to take Gemma to Disneyland. Michael had said that we should ask for the most fantastic things, as all things are the same to the Universe. A big thing is no more difficult or less likely for you to attract than a small thing. So I pondered what would be the most luxurious and fantastical experience I could think of. It was a Greek Island cruise. I incorporated this dream into the technique. This process I understood to be the science behind the power of prayer: "Ask, and it will be given to you; seek, and you will find; knock, and it will be opened to you" (Luke 11:9-10).

After doing this process *several* times over, I received a phone call from Beth, who asked, "What would you say if you were told that you'd won a trip overseas?"

I said, "Well, I'd say thank you very much!"

Beth added, "Think nothing of it."

"What?" I questioned.

"We have just bought three airline tickets to England and the third is for you!"

"But I can't go without Gemma," I quickly clarified.

"Your mother would look after her," Beth resolved.

"Yes, she would, but *I* couldn't be *without* her for *weeks*. If you have a third ticket you need to take your mother with you. Thank you for the lovely thought, but I just couldn't go."

"Ok, if you're sure, we'll give it to Mum then," which was what they did.

This seemed an odd thing for me to do as it was like looking the gift horse in the mouth, and after I had asked for it! Michael had taught that when the Universe brought to you your desire it would be more wonderful than you could have ever imagined and would be the perfect outcome. This offer didn't seem to be that. It had drawbacks so it wasn't the perfect outcome. In faith, I had declined it.

I continued with the techniques and after several weeks had passed my friend Maz phoned. She asked, "What are you doing this time next year?"

"Oh goodness," I sighed, "who knows. Probably much the same as what I am doing now," I added.

"Wrong!" she exclaimed.

"Why, what have you in mind?" I asked.

"I have just come into a little money and *we* are going overseas."

"Really?" I excitedly questioned. "Tell me more."

"Well, I've been wanting to go to Greece to do a 'Shirley Valentine', and I need a travelling companion—and you're it! After that we can go to England and visit your relatives in Kent."

"Maz, I couldn't go without Gemma."

"Of course not; she's coming too! We'll take her to Disneyland. Where else would you like to go?"

"I desperately want to see Hayley."

"*Naturally*!" She said, knowing me so very well.

"We'll slot that in too."

"So when is all this to take place?" I enquired.

"How about this time next year?" she suggested.

"Brilliant," I said. "That will give me time to find some work to get some money together."

"We'll go for three months."

"Three months!" I exclaimed. "I don't know that I should take Gemma out of school for three whole months."

"Well how long do you think then?" she asked.

"More like six weeks I should think."

"Okay then, six weeks it is! I'll pay for all the expenses of travel, accommodation and food," Maz generously offered, "if you can cover your own spending money."

"What an offer! Done deal!" I accepted.

"Find out where and when it suits Hayley to see you and we'll plan the rest of the trip around that."

"Thank you, Maz, that's fabulous."

I was amazed just how quickly work appeared! As soon as our phone call was over, it was time for me to take Gemma's friend home. They had been playing together at our place after school. When I dropped off Gemma's friend, I went in to say hello to her mum, whom I knew through school and through the friendship of our girls. I related to her the turn of events of the last hour and, as I was mentioning about needing to find work, her husband walked into the room and said, "You looking for work, Helen? We have a position available in our office. Why don't you phone the manager in the morning and talk with him. Tell him I told you to phone."

"Thanks, Tommy, I will. Thanks very much!"

I knew that this was Tommy's own business, so saying that he had told me to ring would carry some weight. Indeed it did, and I worked there three days a week right up until I went overseas. This involved having to arrange for Gemma to be looked after before and after school, which I didn't like, but thought that for one year the result would be worth the sacrifice. The firm had wanted me to continue upon my return from our trip but I chose not to, as I wanted to be the one who took Gemma to school and picked her up again. That time was so precious to me. Each day, when she saw me waiting for her inside the school gate on the lawn, she would drop her school bag and run into my open arms and, with the momentum, I would pick her up and swirl her around a couple of times, then put her down and together we would walk back, hand in hand, to pick up her bag. It is times such as those that have been locked into my treasure chest of memories. They mean more than any money could.

The synchronicity of having Tommy offering me this work struck me as amazing. Michael Rowland had been so correct in saying that the Universe will bring your request into manifestation in a far better way than you could ever imagine. How amazing this whole scenario was! The technique had certainly focused my mind onto my desire and subsequently attracted it into my life in a perfect way.

I wrote to Hayley telling her of our planned trip and asked for her suggestion as to when and where we could see her. My desire, and dream, was to visit her in her own home but I didn't have the audacity to ask for that. I left it to pan out as best suited her. She replied that she would be in America during the time of our trip, touring with 'The King and I'. She sent me the itinerary so I could see where she would be at any given time. It seemed that, for us, the most convenient place to see her would be in Chicago. I felt a little disappointed that it wasn't London, but hey, I was going to get to see her again and that was what *really* mattered. I was delighted when Hayley, unexpectedly, sent me CDs of her son's band Kula Shaka. I really loved Crispian's music—as it was a cross between the '60s music of the Beatles and classical Indian music, with very insightful lyrics written by him.

Maz started to put together the outline of the trip and then took it to a travel agent. We needed an around-the-world ticket to incorporate America. As you can't double back on such a ticket it put restrictions on other aspects of the trip. However, as Hayley was the centre pin, we accommodated this. Maz made a tentative booking. She had a few months before she had to confirm with full payment.

Meanwhile, Hayley and I kept in contact. She sent Gemma and me a beautiful publicity photo of herself as Anna, which she had autographed. However, the itinerary of the tour of 'The King and I' had proven to be very tight and demanding, resulting in Hayley having to forfeit the last part of the tour due to exhaustion. I knew that her costume dresses, with the weight of their steel hoops, were very difficult to dance around the stage in. Hayley was of such slight stature that the constancy of the performances, with no time for fatigue-recovery, could well have taken its toll on her health. She had also broken her little toe—twice. That would have proven so difficult for her as dancing in those dresses would require all the help her feet could give. She had to continue only long enough for a replacement Anna to be found.

This changed everything. It was fortunate that we still had a week before we were due to confirm our airline tickets, as now Hayley would be back in London and not Chicago at the time of our trip. So back to the drawing board! We changed our plans, which meant we no longer wanted an around-the-world ticket. The Disneyland venture changed from Anaheim, California to Paris, France (Euro Disney). This was just as great, as Gemma loved the idea of the French language (especially given our French surname) and was definite that she wanted to learn French in high school (she did in fact end up graduating from University with a First Class Honours degree in French [photo 45]).

Communication between Hayley and me dwindled considerably due to her not being well and my not wanting to pressure her. However, our plans were in place, and, as I knew her address in London, I could make written contact with her once we were there as she would be finished with 'The King and I' by then.

I excitedly told friends of our forthcoming trip and that I was going to be able to see Hayley again. Many of them asked if I could get a personalized autographed photo of Hayley for them (most of these requests came from my male friends!) In the end, I had quite a list of such requests. I wasn't sure that I could ask Hayley for all of these as she had better things to do with her time than to sit writing the names of my friends and acquaintances on photos. On the other hand, these were her fans, not just my friends, so she probably wouldn't mind.

I would just have to play it by ear and see if the opportunity presented itself.

The clock ticked on, with the days and weeks passing quickly. When one is busy, the days do seem to rush by. My savings were building according to my plan. When the day came to exchange the saved dollars for travellers' cheques, I had such an exciting sense of achievement. With passports ready, travellers cheques acquired, and luggage being packed, we knew the day of departure was really nearing. Oh, the excitement of it all! Everything I had asked for in my 'mind power' technique I had indeed somehow attracted. It wasn't so much the money that I attracted but rather the experiences that money could give, as I had articulated in the technique. Even Maz's idea to 'do a Shirley Valentine' in Greece had blossomed into a Greek Island Cruise, *without any input from me!* I was in constant amazement at the magic of the power of the mind. It even appeared that, after my initial disappointment, visiting Hayley in her own home was now back in the realm of possibilities.

29) In my first leading role: Mabel in 'Pirates of Penzance', 1975 (aged 15).

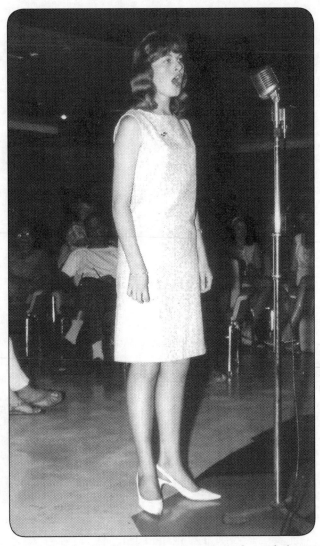

30) Singing 'Edelweis' for the passengers on board the Fairstar, 1966 (aged 16).

31) Duet (centre stage) with Steve Russell, 'Roaring Twenties Night' on board the Fairstar, Dec 1966.

32) With Steve Russell on board the Fairstar.

33) As Rose Maybud in 'Ruddigore', 1967 (aged 17).

34) As Patience in 'Patience', 1968 (aged 18).

35) As Gianetta in 'The Gondoliers', 1969 (aged 19).

36) As Julie Jordan in 'Carousel' (with Dorothea Warburton), 1971 (aged 21).

37) As Cousin Hebe (with Robert White) in 'HMS Pinafore', 1972, (aged 22).

38) As Marianne Beaunoir singing 'Girl on the Prow' in 'New Moon', end of 1972 (aged 23).

39) As Hope Harcourt in 'Anything Goes', 1973 (aged 24).

40) Feathered up for Music Hall (with Dr Alan Cash), Armidale, 1977 (aged 27).

41) Geoff and me during the roller coaster ride of our first time round, 1988.

42) "We Do!" Taking our wedding vows with Fr Stephen Redhead,
Geoff's best friend of 40 years. 22nd April 2006.

43) Oh Happy Day! Husband and wife at last! (Best man, Geoff's elder son, Nathan, with Gemma hidden behind me).

44) With Michael Rowland.

45) Gemma's Graduation photo, April 2010. (Excuse my 'Proud Mum' moment–I wanted to include a more recent picture of my beautiful daughter).

PART EIGHT

Doubt & Divine Timing

Departure day had arrived. Communication with Hayley was at a standstill. I set off in faith that communication between us would be re-established once we were actually in England.

Within the first few days after our arrival in London, Gemma and I went to visit relatives in Kent for two weeks. While we were doing that, Maz and Philip (her partner who was now also travelling with us), took the opportunity of going to their homeland of Scotland. I sent Hayley a letter advising her of our whereabouts and how we could be contacted. The two weeks of our stay passed without any word from Hayley. I was anxious, to say the least, as we were leaving our base for further travelling where contact would not be so easy.

We met up again with Maz and Phil in London, and flew to Athens for the Greek component of our trip. This meant we would not be contactable for the next ten days. I again wrote to Hayley to advise of our movements and where we'd be staying upon our return. We would only be there for a week before leaving again for Paris. I was hoping to see her during that week.

The time in Greece was so wonderful. Our cruise too, although besieged with unseasonable cool, drizzly weather, had been such a fabulous experience. We vowed that we would return sometime in the future, only next time we would 'island hop', allowing us as much time as we desired on each island. We had fallen in love with the Aegean and its island communities.

Mykonos, our last port of call, had brought to us the lovely sunshine as a beautiful finale. Gemma and I braved the cold water to have a swim in the Aegean Sea. It was here that Maz fulfilled her dream of the 'Shirley Valentine' experience, supping on the beachfront, which she included us in. The Aegean backdrop was magical.

I was so grateful for this lovely holiday that Maz had made possible. How could I ever repay her? We had been close friends since we were nine and our friendship certainly was a life-long one [photos 46-47]. We were sorry that the cruise had come to an end just as the weather was improving. However, I was full of anticipation that, upon arriving back at our hotel in London, I would be greeted with a letter from Hayley.

Disappointment overwhelmed me when there was no such letter awaiting me. What was happening here? I knew Hayley too well to think for one minute that she was ignoring me. So, where was she? Was she all right? Was she safe? Was she ill? I was very concerned about her. Again I wrote to her, but this time, being nervous that time was against us, I faxed it to her. The week passed by and we had to leave for Paris without hearing any word from Hayley. I sent another fax advising where we were staying both in the city of Paris and at Euro Disney in the further hope that I would hear from her.

We had a most marvellous time in Paris. Maz and Gemma were brave enough to go to the very top of the Eiffel Tower, but Phil and I chickened out. We had enjoyed a scrumptious and sumptuous luncheon, but it was the bottle of fine wine that, Maz said, had given her the courage to take Gemma to the top. It was a high point (pardon the pun) of Gemma's Paris visit.

We left the Tower and ambled through the colourful city streets. We couldn't get over how many lovers we saw—smooching on park benches, laying on blankets in the park, walking arm in arm, stopping for kisses, standing in everyone's way, oblivious of anyone but themselves. Love was certainly in the air. It certainly confirmed for me that Paris was the City of Love. My thoughts turned to Geoff.

The four days spent at Euro Disney were a dream-come-true. We stayed within the Euro Disney compound, but outside the Euro Disney Theme Park. Our accommodation was in the Annie Oakley building of the Cheyenne Hotel, which was situated within the Wild-West themed quarters. Each day, we walked along a canal, passing by tepees and other western-themed artefacts on our way to the Entrance Gates of Euro Disney.

Our time spent at Disneyland each day was filled with adventure. It was very exciting, not just for Gemma, but also for me. I had been an enthusiastic Mouseketeer when I was nine, back in the late 50s, owning Mouseketeer ears (which I still have), the blue pleated skirt, and the Mickey Mouse Club polo-necked t-shirt with my name on the front and the Club logo on the back [photo 48]. Mum had taken me to the Tennis Stadium to see the Mouseketeers when they had visited Sydney. I had regularly watched the Mickey Mouse Club on TV and seen the Mouseketeers visiting Disneyland and riding in the teacups. How I had yearned to experience that for myself. And here I was, almost forty years later, achieving that dream [photo 49]. Talk about a second childhood! It was lovely that I could experience this with my ten-year-old daughter [photo 50].

Each evening upon our return to the hotel, I was hopeful that there might be a letter from Hayley awaiting me. There wasn't. We spent another night back in Paris prior to our journey back to London. Again, there was no letter awaiting me! We boarded the train for London the next morning (travelling under the English Channel, which added further adventure to our holiday), but I had heaviness in my heart. I was banking on the fact that there would be a letter awaiting me when we arrived back at our hotel. The conclusion of our trip was closing in on me and I started to feel desperate. I couldn't believe that I had come all this way and would have to end up going home to Australia not having met up with Hayley—the first and foremost reason that I had worked so hard to manifest this trip.

A thought came to me! If the power of the mind had brought me this far, perhaps applying it again would reap the result I so longed for. I employed a visioning technique, taught by Michael Rowland, of my receiving a letter from Hayley. I was cross with myself for not having thought to do so earlier.

As we alighted from the taxi, I left the others behind in my rush to get to the reception desk before it closed. Was there a letter for me? *No.* My world came crashing down. Tears welled as I turned to help the others with our luggage. I couldn't believe it! All the energy I had put into attracting this trip, so we could get to see Hayley again, seemed to have been wasted. We went to our rooms to freshen up before regrouping for dinner.

The planning of our last week in England was the topic of discussion at dinner. It was an open page. Maz had friends in Denmark whom she thought she would like to visit and suggested we all go there. Phil was keen, but I was heavy-hearted at the thought of leaving London. We had eight days left before flying home and I just couldn't risk not being here during the last possible opportunity of hearing from Hayley. Gemma wanted to do 'something exciting', so, I suggested that Maz and Phil visited Denmark, while Gemma and I stayed in the budget hotel and had day trips out into the London tourist spots yet unexplored by us. Everyone was happy with this outcome.

So it was that, each day, Gemma and I enjoyed an outing. We visited Harrods, just for the experience, and bought a couple of Harrods souvenirs. We also went to Hamleys Toy Store, where we spent hours perusing the intriguing merchandise on each of the seven toy-packed floors. Gemma was particularly interested in the magic section as she had enjoyed exploring this art on the cruise ship. There had been magicians performing for us on the cruise and they had offered a workshop for passengers to attend. Gemma and another girl, whom she had palled up with, went along and were captivated. They came away from it with several tricks up their sleeves with which to amaze us. Gemma had been performing them for everyone. Here at Hamleys, Gemma saw a magic box that she really wanted. However, it was more than I could afford to spend on that day, but promised that, if we had enough money left over on the day before leaving for home, we could come back and buy it. I was being pretty careful with my spending.

We visited Madame Tussaud's Waxworks Museum, which was also a big hit with us both. The model of Van Gogh was Gemma's favourite as she was studying him at school; my favourite was Einstein as the likeness to photos of him was amazing and the figure was so life-like. We visited the Planetarium, which was fantastic (yet so humbling—being confronted by the amazing vastness of Space jolted me into an awareness of how insignificant we appear in the bigger scheme of things). We walked down the Mall to Buckingham Palace and saw the changing of the guard, and later picnicked on the grass in a very pretty garden nearby. We were making the most of every day.

I had come to understand that I was not going to get to see Hayley, but I was not very good at accepting or believing this fact. I worried about her. Although I did enjoy my days out with Gemma, I was heavy of heart. *How could this happen? After all the planning around seeing Hayley! How is it that I had attracted everything else about this trip, yet the most important part hadn't manifested?* I can't describe the disappointment I felt. It was now Friday evening and we were flying home on Tuesday. At this point I accepted the unlikeliness of it happening within the last three days of our time in London. My anxiety and resistance fell away with this recognition and in its place came resignation.

Gemma and I arrived back at our hotel after an exhausting day walking around London. As we entered the foyer my eyes spotted an envelope pinned on the notice board. On closer inspection, I found that it was addressed to me . . . *and it was in Hayley's handwriting*! Such relief! I tore it open and eagerly read her letter. It explained everything! She had been so exhausted after 'The King and I' tour, and so close to having a break-down that she had been on an enforced holiday in the States for rest and recuperation before being well enough to fly back to London. She had only just arrived back and found all my desperate correspondence. She had written her telephone number in the letter so that I could phone her.

With only three days left before our flight out on the fourth day, I wasted no time that evening in phoning her. Hayley was so sorry that I had felt such anxiety, but was relieved that there still was time to get together. She was still feeling weak and unwell so it was only right that I offered to come to her, rather than her having to come into London to us. Hayley appreciated this and invited us to come to *her home* and have lunch together on Sunday. *Yes!*

We chatted a little and arranged that I would let her know what time our train would be arriving at Hampton Station so she could be there to meet us. As we were bringing our conversation to a close, I said how grateful I was that I didn't have to leave England without seeing her. Hayley agreed that it was a close call, but at least it was happening. After making enquiries the next morning, I was able to phone her back with the train timetable details. Plans made, I only had to wait 'one more sleep' before meeting up with her again—*at her home!* It seemed that once I had let go of the desperation for the desired outcome, which had held resistance, the right vibrational energy of non-resistance arose, allowing the desired manifestation to take place.

The following morning I bounced out of bed with such spring in my step that I reminded myself of Tigger. Gemma too was very excited. She was going to see Hayley in the role as her 'godmother' for the first time. We headed off on our journey to Hayley. I was full of such excitement and anticipation that I was almost giddy. Upon seeing the Hampton Station sign on the platform as the train slowed in its approach, a wave of flutters surged through me. Any moment now we would be seeing Hayley again. We alighted from the train and looked around but there was no Hayley to be seen. Just then I noticed her getting out of her car at the entrance to the station. "There she is, Gemma. Come on," I urged. We hurried toward her.

"You made it, Helen! How wonderful!" were Hayley's words of welcome and cheer as my darling daughter and I kissed and embraced her. This was the *par excellence* of a dream come true. Then, for her to be driving us in her Mercedes to her tree-hidden, two-hundred-year-old home was beyond realism. *Surely I am dreaming all of this! How could this be happening to me? How is it that I am here living this dream?* The little insignificant mouse had morphed into a powerful being—so powerful that I was living in a whirlwind of fantasy. This was absurd!

Before I knew it, we had pulled up at her door and *I was being welcomed into Hayley Mills' home as her friend.* My mind glimpsed back at the day in 1986 when I had been given the magazine article on her home. The last paragraph of the article had said that she enjoyed having friends over for lunch on Sundays and it had caused me to think that I should be one of those friends. *Now here I was—and it was Sunday!* This reality struck me with awe. I stepped through the magazine pages right into her home.

As we entered through the front door into Hayley's private world, I was trying so hard to act composed, when in fact I was totally overcome with the reality of the moment. Again my mind glimpsed back at my bedroom wall, full of Hayley's photos, and I recalled how I had known then of my connection with her, but not been able to understand it. I felt the joy of 'being at home again' with my long lost sister for whom I had felt so much grief in my past life, which I had brought forward into this life. At this moment I felt a wave of healing roll through my body.

My thoughts were interrupted by Hayley's voice offering us to come through into the family room. The walls of this room were full of photo frames containing amazing photographs of special moments in the life and times of Hayley Mills. She and her family featured in several of the photos in the company of some of the most famous thespians of our era. Of course, *they themselves* were some of the famous thespians of our era. It was such a privilege to be shown this gallery of treasured photos.

Hayley took us out into her lovely back garden, where we took some photos [photos 51-52]. There were some particularly beautiful rosebuds in bloom so I asked Hayley if I could take a photo of her with them [photo 53]. I love this photo. Hayley then took us through a gate in the back hedge that led into another garden area. It was a natural garden of wildflowers, very different from the kept flowerbeds. This was like a secret garden, beyond the obvious garden. After a time in this beautiful sanctuary of flowers and birdsong, we went back indoors.

We chatted in the kitchen while Hayley made a pot of tea. Then we adjourned into a room that was a very private and personal room. In hindsight I think it was her study, although at the time I just thought of it as a sitting room. It was very cosy and welcoming. It housed the telephone and fax machine, her desk with some papers on it, bookshelves, some books and a small vase of roses on a coffee table, and a few comfy chairs in which we sat as the three of us engaged in conversation.

At one point the phone rang, which progressed to the fax machine. Hayley picked up the faxed message and stood for a moment reading it. I said, "If there is something you need to attend to, please do. We can wait." She turned the page around and held it up for our perusal. Her face beamed as we silently read, "I LOVE YOU & MISS YOU". It was obvious that her heart was melting as she continued to tell us about her new love, Firdous. Her face glowed as she spoke of him. I felt so wonderfully happy for her. She explained that Firdous was also part of the cast of 'The King and I' tour, and that without his loving arms she was sure she would have actually experienced a collapse. He was now back home in New York, and there was an Atlantic Ocean between them. It was obviously very hard on them both. Hayley and I were sharing together on a level that we had in our letters over the intervening years. We really did have a true friendship.

As lunchtime neared, Hayley said that she had intended taking us over to her parents' home for lunch but that her father had phoned earlier saying that her mother was not having a good day with her dementia and that to bring people into the home, whom she didn't know, would be far too confusing for her to cope with. I was amazed that Hayley had thought to take us home to her parents. If I hadn't already felt that total friendship from Hayley, I certainly did so now. It really quite stunned me how embracing of us she was. Instead, she suggested that we go to the local pub for lunch. We were very happy indeed to do this, so we piled back into her Mercedes and drove a short distance into the village.

Once there we were advised that Gemma couldn't come in, even just to eat, as she was under age. That hadn't crossed our minds. So we ordered and sat outside at a table sheltered by an umbrella. Gemma was off enjoying herself with the several large ornaments adorning the front of the pub, which gave way for Hayley and me to get into some nitty-gritty dialogue. We had such deep and meaningful discussions on all sorts of topics.

Hayley was very empathetic over my pining for my lost love, and she gave me very good and wise counsel.

The wind was gathering a little strength that was not conducive to our comfort. So, after eating our meal, we made a hasty retreat back to the comfort of Hayley's sitting room. It was a shame that the wind had caused our conversation to be cut short as, once back at Hayley's home, we didn't resume the same level of sharing that we had been enjoying—it was not for Gemma's ears, and we wanted to include her in what we were doing and talking about.

Gemma performed her magic tricks for Hayley, who responded with genuine amazement. Gemma really was very good at them. I told Hayley of the magic box at Hamleys and how we hoped to go back to buy it for her. We then talked about the books we were reading, and Hayley asked if I had read Marianne Williamson's new book 'A Woman's Worth'. I said that I didn't even know about it. With hearing that, she said she thought she had a spare copy upstairs and excused herself to go and fetch it. Upon her return, she handed it to me. I started to peruse it thinking she was just showing it to me, when suddenly I noticed that she had inscribed the title page to me [photo 54]. Realizing that she was giving it to me as a gift I jumped up out of my seat and hugged her. She said that it was her pleasure and hoped I got as much out of it as she had. Then she turned to Gemma and said, "And I want you to have that magic box so here's the money to buy it," and handed her a fifty pound note! I was more taken aback than even Gemma was. Thanking her, Gemma threw her arms around Hayley's neck and kissed her. I said, "Oh, Hayley, that's so generous—thank you."

"Well," said Hayley, "she *is* my darling goddaughter."

One more cup of tea and our time was drawing to an end. Hayley pulled out some photos from her desk drawer and proceeded to write on them for us. She inscribed a photo for me with *Dearest Helen, love and light little sister, Hayley xx.* Seeing these photos jogged my memory about the list of people who had asked me to bring them back autographed photos. Sheepishly, I asked Hayley if she would mind signing several more for my friends who had asked for them. She was rather flattered that they were wanted and happily sat there signing away as I reeled off the names for her. I ended up with a tidy little bundle of about twelve to take home to delight those who had asked for them.

Once this autographing session was complete, it was time for Hayley to take us back to the station. Although our day with Hayley was coming to an end I couldn't feel sad as I was so full of joy from being with her again and from having had the experience of visiting her in her home. I took a last minute photo of Hayley and Gemma outside the front of Hayley's home, and turned and took one of the driveway [photos 55-56]. We hurriedly bundled ourselves back into the Mercedes and drove away from the experience that I had dreamed of for years. As we drove down the long, tree-lined entrance, which hid Hayley's home from the road, I revelled in the wondrous privilege it had been to be invited there. We had been totally accepted as trusted and loving friends and it was obvious that our bond from our past life was now very real in this one.

Hayley had been so gracious. She had given us such a lovely day even though she was feeling so unwell. It had been apparent from my desperate correspondence just how important meeting up with her again was to me and she had obviously put that ahead of her own feelings of being unwell, and had done so with love. I had such gratitude for all she had given to us this day. She was indeed everything I had ever believed her to be. She exuded loving kindness. I was more convinced now than ever of her connection with the God-essence within.

We arrived at the station and Hayley pulled up near the entrance, as parking spots were not easy to find. We exchanged our fond farewells and expressed our heartfelt thanks. As we walked through the entrance of the station I turned back and watched as Hayley drove away. I sent up a prayer of gratitude and of blessing upon her.

We sat at the railway station, spellbound; my arms wrapped around Gemma. Her head rested on my shoulder; my head rested back onto hers. I was reeling in the afterglow of a dream come true.

Two shall be born
the whole wide world apart
and these over unknown seas
to unknown lands
shall bend each wondering step
to this one end . . . .
That one day out of darkness
they shall meet
and read life's meaning
in each other's eyes.

Suzan Marr Spalding

46) Maz and me at her property in the Hunter Valley of NSW in 2000.

47) A beautiful photo of Maz taken on board the 'Olympic Princess' during our Greek Island cruise, 1998.

48) Mouseketeer Helen in 1959 (aged 10).

49) Living out my childhood dream (and my second childhood)
in the teacups at Disneyland, Paris.

50) Sharing the Disneyland adventure with Gemma and Mickey.

51) Gemma and Hayley in Hayley's rose garden.

52) Hayley and me together in her garden.

53) A very treasured photo: One I took of Hayley
in her rose garden.*

**54) Hayley's inscription to me in the book 'A Woman's Worth'
by Marianne Williamson.**

55) Hayley's London home at the time.

56) Hayley's tree-lined driveway. An apt photo with which to close the book as it depicts the ending of the day that culminated in my dream-coming-true.

Bonus For Purchasers of this book:

* Photos marked * can be obtained in colour, as a set of 15, in PDF form, by visitng www.FindingHayleyFindingMe.com.au and requesting them through the 'Contact' page, and quoting the last word on page 22 of this book.